Deregulation

Other Books of Related Interest:

Opposing Viewpoints Series

The Banking Crisis

At Issue Series

Are America's Wealthy Too Powerful?

Current Controversies Series

The World Economy

"Congress shall make no law ... abridging the freedom of speech, or of the press."

First Amendment to the U.S. Constitution

The basic foundation of our democracy is the First Amendment guarantee of freedom of expression. The Opposing Viewpoints Series is dedicated to the concept of this basic freedom and the idea that it is more important to practice it than to enshrine it.

Deregulation

Dedria Bryfonski, Book Editor

GREENHAVEN PRESS
A part of Gale, Cengage Learning

GALE
CENGAGE Learning

Detroit • New York • San Francisco • New Haven, Conn • Waterville, Maine • London

Christine Nasso, *Publisher*
Elizabeth Des Chenes, *Managing Editor*

© 2011 Greenhaven Press, a part of Gale, Cengage Learning.

Gale and Greenhaven Press are registered trademarks used herein under license.

For more information, contact:
Greenhaven Press
27500 Drake Rd.
Farmington Hills, MI 48331-3535
Or you can visit our Internet site at gale.cengage.com

For product information and technology assistance, contact us at

Gale Customer Support, 1-800-877-4253
For permission to use material from this text or product, submit all requests online at www.cengage.com/permissions

Further permissions questions can be emailed to permissionrequest@cengage.com

Articles in Greenhaven Press anthologies are often edited for length to meet page requirements. In addition, original titles of these works are changed to clearly present the main thesis and to explicitly indicate the author's opinion. Every effort is made to ensure that Greenhaven Press accurately reflects the original intent of the authors. Every effort has been made to trace the owners of copyrighted material.

Cover Image copyright fotohunter, 2010. Used under license from Shutterstock.com.

LIBRARY OF CONGRESS CATALOGING-IN-PUBLICATION DATA

Deregulation / Dedria Bryfonski, book editor.
 p. cm. -- (Opposing viewpoints)
 Includes bibliographical references and index.
 ISBN 978-0-7377-5108-6 (hardcover) -- ISBN 978-0-7377-5109-3 (pbk.)
 1. Deregulation--United States--Juvenile literature. 2. Industrial policy--United States--Juvenile literature. 3. Trade regulation--United States--Juvenile literature. I. Bryfonski, Dedria.
 HD3616.U47D425 2010
 338.973--dc22

 2010030776

3 1907 00269 0435

Printed in the United States of America
1 2 3 4 5 6 7 14 13 12 11 10

Contents

Chapter 3: Should Certain Industries Be Deregulated?

Chapter 4: How Has Deregulation Affected the Global Economy?

Why Consider
Opposing Viewpoints?

> *"The only way in which a human being can make some approach to knowing the whole of a subject is by hearing what can be said about it by persons of every variety of opinion and studying all modes in which it can be looked at by every character of mind. No wise man ever acquired his wisdom in any mode but this."*
>
> John Stuart Mill

In our media-intensive culture it is not difficult to find differing opinions. Thousands of newspapers and magazines and dozens of radio and television talk shows resound with differing points of view. The difficulty lies in deciding which opinion to agree with and which "experts" seem the most credible. The more inundated we become with differing opinions and claims, the more essential it is to hone critical reading and thinking skills to evaluate these ideas. Opposing Viewpoints books address this problem directly by presenting stimulating debates that can be used to enhance and teach these skills. The varied opinions contained in each book examine many different aspects of a single issue. While examining these conveniently edited opposing views, readers can develop critical thinking skills such as the ability to compare and contrast authors' credibility, facts, argumentation styles, use of persuasive techniques, and other stylistic tools. In short, the Opposing Viewpoints Series is an ideal way to attain the higher-level thinking and reading skills so essential in a culture of diverse and contradictory opinions.

In addition to providing a tool for critical thinking, Opposing Viewpoints books challenge readers to question their own strongly held opinions and assumptions. Most people form their opinions on the basis of upbringing, peer pressure, and personal, cultural, or professional bias. By reading carefully balanced opposing views, readers must directly confront new ideas as well as the opinions of those with whom they disagree. This is not to simplistically argue that everyone who reads opposing views will—or should—change his or her opinion. Instead, the series enhances readers' understanding of their own views by encouraging confrontation with opposing ideas. Careful examination of others' views can lead to the readers' understanding of the logical inconsistencies in their own opinions, perspective on why they hold an opinion, and the consideration of the possibility that their opinion requires further evaluation.

Evaluating Other Opinions

To ensure that this type of examination occurs, Opposing Viewpoints books present all types of opinions. Prominent spokespeople on different sides of each issue as well as well-known professionals from many disciplines challenge the reader. An additional goal of the series is to provide a forum for other, less known, or even unpopular viewpoints. The opinion of an ordinary person who has had to make the decision to cut off life support from a terminally ill relative, for example, may be just as valuable and provide just as much insight as a medical ethicist's professional opinion. The editors have two additional purposes in including these less known views. One, the editors encourage readers to respect others' opinions—even when not enhanced by professional credibility. It is only by reading or listening to and objectively evaluating others' ideas that one can determine whether they are worthy of consideration. Two, the inclusion of such viewpoints encourages the important critical thinking skill of objectively evaluating an author's credentials and bias. This evaluation will illuminate an author's reasons for taking a particular stance on an issue and will aid in readers' evaluation of the author's ideas.

It is our hope that these books will give readers a deeper understanding of the issues debated and an appreciation of the complexity of even seemingly simple issues when good and honest people disagree. This awareness is particularly important in a democratic society such as ours in which people enter into public debate to determine the common good. Those with whom one disagrees should not be regarded as enemies but rather as people whose views deserve careful examination and may shed light on one's own.

Thomas Jefferson once said that "difference of opinion leads to inquiry, and inquiry to truth." Jefferson, a broadly educated man, argued that "if a nation expects to be ignorant and free ... it expects what never was and never will be." As individuals and as a nation, it is imperative that we consider the opinions of others and examine them with skill and discernment. The Opposing Viewpoints Series is intended to help readers achieve this goal.

David L. Bender and Bruno Leone,
Founders

Introduction

> "The government's view of the economy could be summed up in a few short phrases: If it moves, tax it. If it keeps moving, regulate it. And if it stops moving, subsidize it."
>
> Ronald Reagan,
> president of the United States, 1981–89

> "The cause of the current troubles dates back to 1980, when U.S. President Ronald Reagan and U.K. Prime Minister Margaret Thatcher came to power. . . . These leaders believed that markets are self-correcting, meaning that if prices get out of whack, they will eventually revert to historical norms. Instead, this laissez-faire attitude created the current housing bubble, which in turn led to the seizing up of credit markets."
>
> George Soros,
> Hungarian American businessman
> and activist

On April 21, 2010, President Barack Obama took his appeal for financial regulatory reform to arguably his toughest audience, Wall Street bankers, in an address at Cooper Union in Manhattan. "Unless your business model depends on bilking people, there is little to fear from these new rules," he said. As top executives from leading banks nationally and internationally sat in mostly stony silence, the president chided them for their "failure of responsibility" that created the financial crisis.

Also in the audience was Michael Bloomberg, the mayor of New York City and the founder and majority owner of Bloomberg L.P., an information provider serving the financial industry. In an interview on MSNBC, Bloomberg suggested that the president and Congress are overreacting based on a desire to assuage popular anger at the financial industry. "The real danger here is that we write a bill based on populist reaction—'I'm gonna get the SOBs'—because of a financial crisis which incidentally they . . . had something to do with but were not the only ones responsible for," Bloomberg said. In his role as mayor, Bloomberg says he is concerned that the financial reform bill will negatively impact jobs and profits in the financial sector.

The landmark financial reform bill that was signed into law by President Obama in July 2010—the most sweeping financial reform since the Great Depression—was created to avoid a repeat of the events that led to the financial crisis. The financial crisis that came to a head in September 2008 was caused by the collapse of the U.S. housing market and the subsequent devaluation of many investment instruments whose underlying assets were mortgages. The controversial piece of legislation has five major components:

- A council of federal regulators, led by the treasury secretary, will monitor the level of risk within the financial system.

- The amount of debt that banks are allowed to take on is reduced, to improve their solvency.

- If a financial institution fails, the council of federal regulators has the power to dispose of the institution in an orderly manner. The government will take over the institution and run it until its assets can be broken off and sold.

- A Consumer Financial Protection Agency, housed in the Federal Reserve, is created to prevent abusive lending practices, especially in the mortgage market.

- Regulators are granted authority over a wider range of financial institutions, including the derivatives marketplace.

In addition to the concerns raised by Mr. Bloomberg, many Republicans and bankers also take issue with the act, with their concerns falling into the following categories:

- The Federal Reserve Board failed to predict the financial crisis and acted unwisely in the recent financial crisis. Giving them more authority will not help matters if they continue to act inappropriately.

- Forcing banks to reduce their debt means they have less money to loan to consumers and businesses, thus impeding economic recovery.

- The plan provides assurances that the government will bail out any future bank failures, thus encouraging risky behavior by financial institutions and putting taxpayers on the hook for future bailouts.

- The Consumer Financial Protection Agency will constrain consumers' choices.

- The additional regulations will increase bureaucracy, stifle innovation, and make the U.S. economy less competitive globally.

How did the United States get to this point? Undeniably the recent financial regulatory reform was prompted by the financial crisis that came to a crescendo in September 2008. In this way, it closely resembles the history of the Great Depression—in each instance, an era marked by a deregulatory philosophy is followed by a period of regulation. Although the regulations following the Great Depression were far-reaching, they were also fragmented. Instead of an omnibus regulatory act investing oversight in a centralized, coordinated factor, a series of acts regulated individual financial activities. These included the following:

- In 1933, the Securities Act of 1933 required businesses to register the initial offer or sale of a security[1] with the government. The Federal Home Loan Bank Board was set up to oversee savings and loan institutions. The Glass-Steagall Act separated banks into either commercial banks or investment banks. Commercial banks engaged in traditional deposit account and loan activities, while investment banks engaged in riskier trading activities.

- In 1934, the Securities and Exchange Commission (SEC) was formed to regulate the stock exchange. Publically traded firms were required to submit quarterly and annual financial reports to the SEC.

- In 1936, the Commodity Exchange Act was established to set rules of trading commodities and futures.

A philosophy favorable to financial regulation remained until the 1970s, when the work of economist Milton Friedman, among others, on the benefits of free market capitalism gained ascendancy. Friedman advocated reducing government regulations and restraints on business, allowing free market forces to prevail. Under laissez-faire capitalism, as barriers to competition are removed, a survival of the fittest scenario occurs, with the stronger companies prevailing. Consolidation frequently occurs, resulting in fewer, but more financially stable, businesses. These businesses are more productive and efficient than the failing businesses and are able to invest some of their increased profits in the form of lower prices and improved services for consumers.

The presidency of Ronald Reagan and the nearly thirty-year reign of Alan Greenspan as chairman of the Federal Reserve Board did much to speed the spread of deregulation in the United States. Both were strong supporters of a free market economy created by a loosening of regulations. From the 1970s on, a number of industries, including transportation, energy, telecommunications, and airlines, were deregulated. Additionally, during this same time frame, a series of laws were enacted that reduced regulation in the financial industry. Some of these acts included:

- In 1980, among other provisions, the Depository Institutions Deregulation and Monetary Control Act allowed banks to merge and also eliminated a cap on interest rates in savings and other deposit accounts.

- In 1982, the Garn-St. Germain Depository Institutions Act deregulated the savings and loan industry and is blamed for setting the stage for the savings and loan crisis of the late 1980s.

- In 1994, the Riegle-Neal Interstate Banking and Branching Efficiency Act eliminated restrictions on interstate banking. This resulted in a consolidation of banks, as stronger banks were able to compete in new markets.

- In 1999, the Gramm-Leach-Bliley Act repealed the Glass-Steagall Act, allowing traditional commercial banks to engage in investment banking activities.

- In 2000, the Commodity Futures Modernization Act precluded derivatives[2] from being regulated by the Commodity Futures Trading Commission.

- In 2004, the SEC decreased cash in reserve requirements for banks, which led to an increase in the debt levels of many banks.

The role that these deregulatory acts played in the financial crisis that unfolded in 2008, as well as the validity of deregulation as a financial policy, is a subject of intense debate. The viewpoints of supporters and those opposed to deregulation are presented in the following chapters: Did Deregulation Cause the Financial Crisis? Is Greater Regulation Needed to Prevent Another Financial Crisis? Should Certain Industries Be Deregulated? and How Has Deregulation Affected the Global Economy?

Notes

1. A security is a financial instrument representing ownership in the issuing organization. The most common form of security is stock in a publicly traded company. However, other securities include bonds, derivatives, or shares in an investment fund.

2. Derivatives have no underlying financial worth but are instead financial products with worth based on changes in the value of the underlying asset. Underlying assets usually consist of stocks or groupings of stocks in an index, a specific financial event, interest rates, or commodities. Participants in derivatives are essentially wagering that the asset will either grow or decline and that they will be paid or lose their investment based on the behavior of the asset.

OPPOSING
VIEWPOINTS®
SERIES

CHAPTER 1

Did Deregulation Cause the Financial Crisis?

Chapter Preface

Goldman Sachs is one of the world's largest investment banking and financial services firms, with revenues of more than $45 billion in 2009. It suffered, as did many financial institutions, during the global credit crisis in 2008 and accepted federal funds. In 2009, however, it had its most profitable year in history and was the first bank to pay back the federal loans. Executive bonuses that seemed to some excessive and unseemly for a company that had accepted federal aid were paid out for 2008 performance, causing a public outcry against the company. The company became a lightning rod for public outrage about abusive Wall Street practices.

Goldman Sachs again found itself the target of unwelcome publicity when, in April 2010, the U.S. Securities and Exchange Commission (SEC) charged the company with fraud for creating and selling a mortgage investment that was designed to fail. According to SEC charges, a Goldman employee helped Paulson & Co., a hedge fund[1] managed by John Paulson, set up a collateralized debt obligation[2] so that the hedge fund could short[3] it—essentially betting that the securities[4] in the instrument would decline in value. Goldman and the hedge fund sold the security to investors without disclosing that the whole security had been designed to fail, the SEC alleged. In a Senate hearing following the SEC charges, Goldman Sachs's chief executive officer testified that the company had no moral obligation to inform clients that the company was betting against products it was selling. The Goldman Sachs story is one at the center of the bank reform debate—did lax regulation of complex financial instruments contribute to the financial crisis?

According to Zach Carter in an April 20, 2010, article titled "How Deregulation Fueled Goldman's Scam" posted on the Web site AlterNet, the answer is a resounding yes:

Better derivatives[5] regulations could help protect against fraud. If Goldman Sachs'[s] sketchy subprime[6] deal had been subject to market scrutiny on an exchange, it's very unlikely that any investor would have bought into it. Goldman Sachs almost got away with it because the deal was secretive and beyond the scope of most regulatory oversight. . . . It's abundantly clear that almost every major regulatory agency charged with curtailing financial excess failed to prevent the Crash of 2008. But that failure doesn't mean that effective regulation is impossible—it only shows that the *regulators* in power failed.

Warren Buffett, a legendary investor and the third-richest man in the world in 2010, who is also a shareholder of Goldman Sachs, takes a contrary view. To Buffett, the relevant fact is not who put the deal together; it is up to each individual investor to do due diligence to assess the deal. "I don't care if John Paulson is shorting these bonds. I'm going to have no worries that he has superior knowledge. It's our job to assess the credit."

The Goldman Sachs case highlights issues surrounding deregulation and its role in the fiscal crisis. In the following chapter, analysts and commentators voice their opinions on the role deregulation may have played in the crisis.

Notes

1. A hedge fund is a private investment pool characterized by unconventional investment methods and minimal regulation. These funds typically undertake balanced risks to ensure profit regardless of market conditions.
2. In collateralized debt obligations (CDOs), a collection of loans or bonds are pooled together into a financial product that is then sold as a separate investment. Typically, in a CDO, one institution will make a loan and then sell the loan to another financial institution, such as an investment bank. The investment bank pools loans into financial products that are sold to investors. The original loans can be

mortgages, auto loans, corporate debt, or credit card debt. The products are divided into risk categories, and investors in the safest categories are paid off before those in the highest risk categories, as the borrowers pay off their debts.

3. "Selling short" is a term used when an investor enters a financial arrangement betting that an asset will decline in value. Typically, an investor will identify a financial instrument such as a stock or derivative and have his broker "lend" the stock to him, with the broker selling a stock from the broker's account to a third party and crediting the proceeds to the investor's account. At some point, the investor needs to pay off the loan to the broker and will pay back the value of the stock at present. If the stock has declined in value, the investor pays the broker less than he was originally credited, and thus makes money on the transaction, even though the stock is worth less.

4. A security is a financial instrument representing ownership in the issuing organization. The most common form of security is stock in a publicly traded company. Other securities include bonds, derivatives, or shares in an investment fund.

5. Derivatives have no underlying financial worth but are instead financial products with worth based on changes in the value of the underlying asset. Underlying assets usually consist of stocks or groupings of stocks in an index, a specific financial event, interest rates, or commodities. Participants in derivatives are essentially wagering that the asset will either grow or decline and that they will be paid or lose their investment based on the behavior of the asset.

6. Subprime mortgages are designed for individuals with poor credit; these loan agreements are more risky than prime mortgages for lenders and more expensive for borrowers.

| "The truth is most of the individual mistakes boil down to just one: a belief that markets are self-adjusting and that the role of government should be minimal."

Deregulation Caused the Financial Crisis

Joseph E. Stiglitz

Joseph E. Stiglitz is a professor of economics at Columbia University. He received the Nobel Prize in Economics in 2001.

Stiglitz contends in the following viewpoint that underlying the financial crisis were five key decisions stemming from a flawed economic philosophy that lasted from the Ronald Reagan administration through the George W. Bush administration. The first was replacing Paul Volcker, a regulator, as chairman of the Federal Reserve Board with Alan Greenspan, a deregulator. The second was the repeal of the Glass-Steagall Act; by allowing commercial banks to also act as investment banks, Stiglitz argues, a culture of risk taking was introduced to these formerly conservative institutions. The third action was the Bush tax cuts, which set the stage for excessive borrowing by the American public. The fourth was the decision not to address stock options in the Sarbanes-Oxley Act, thus creating a structure that gave senior executives an incentive to exaggerate earnings. And the fifth, according to Stiglitz, was a bank bailout that failed to address the real issues causing the crisis—a flawed incentive system and inadequate regulations.

As you read, consider the following questions:

1. According to Stiglitz, what were some of the actions that Alan Greenspan, as chairman of the Federal Reserve Board, could have done to ease the effects of the high-tech and housing bubbles?

2. Why does Stiglitz believe the tax cuts of 2001 and 2003 helped set the stage for the financial crisis?

3. With the economy weakening, why was reliance on exports only a short-term solution, according to the author?

There will come a moment when the most urgent threats posed by the credit crisis have eased and the larger task before us will be to chart a direction for the economic steps ahead. This will be a dangerous moment. Behind the debates over future policy is a debate over history—a debate over the causes of our current situation. The battle for the past will determine the battle for the present. So it's crucial to get the history straight.

What were the critical decisions that led to the crisis? Mistakes were made at every fork in the road—we had what engineers call a "system failure," when not a single decision but a cascade of decisions produce a tragic result. Let's look at five key moments.

No. 1: Firing the Chairman

In 1987 the [Ronald] Reagan administration decided to remove Paul Volcker as chairman of the Federal Reserve Board [the Fed] and appoint Alan Greenspan in his place. Volcker had done what central bankers are supposed to do. On his watch, inflation had been brought down from more than 11 percent to under 4 percent. In the world of central banking, that should have earned him a grade of A+++ and assured his re-appointment. But Volcker also understood that financial markets need to be regulated. Reagan wanted someone who did not believe any such thing, and he found him in a devotee of the objectivist philosopher and free-market zealot Ayn Rand.

Greenspan played a double role. The Fed controls the money spigot, and in the early years of this decade, he turned it on full force. But the Fed is also a regulator. If you appoint an anti-regulator as your enforcer, you know what kind of en-forcement you'll get. A flood of liquidity combined with the failed levees of regulation proved disastrous.

Greenspan presided over not one but two financial bubbles. After the high-tech bubble popped, in 2000–2001, he helped inflate the housing bubble. The first responsibility of a central bank should be to maintain the stability of the finan-cial system. If banks lend on the basis of artificially high asset prices, the result can be a meltdown—as we are seeing now, and as Greenspan should have known. He had many of the tools he needed to cope with the situation. To deal with the high-tech bubble, he could have increased margin require-ments (the amount of cash people need to put down to buy stock). To deflate the housing bubble, he could have curbed predatory lending to low-income households and prohibited other insidious practices (the no-documentation—or "liar"—loans, the interest-only loans, and so on). This would have gone a long way toward protecting us. If he didn't have the tools, he could have gone to Congress and asked for them.

Of course, the current problems with our financial system are not solely the result of bad lending. The banks have made mega-bets with one another through complicated instruments such as derivatives,[1] credit default swaps,[2] and so forth. With these, one party pays another if certain events happen—for instance, if Bear Stearns goes bankrupt, or if the dollar soars. These instruments were originally created to help manage risk—but they can also be used to gamble. Thus, if you felt confident that the dollar was going to fall, you could make a big bet accordingly, and if the dollar indeed fell, your profits would soar. The problem is that, with this complicated intertwining of bets of great magnitude, no one could be sure of the financial position of anyone else—or even of one's own position. Not surprisingly, the credit markets froze.

Here too Greenspan played a role. When I was chairman of the Council of Economic Advisers, during the [Bill] Clinton administration, I served on a committee of all the major federal financial regulators, a group that included Greenspan and Treasury Secretary Robert Rubin. Even then, it was clear that derivatives posed a danger. We didn't put it as memorably as [successful investor] Warren Buffett—who saw derivatives as "financial weapons of mass destruction"—but we took his point. And yet, for all the risk, the deregulators in charge of the financial system—at the Fed, at the Securities and Exchange Commission [SEC], and elsewhere—decided to do nothing, worried that any action might interfere with "innovation" in the financial system. But innovation, like "change," has no inherent value. It can be bad (the "liar" loans are a good example) as well as good.

No. 2: Tearing Down the Walls

The deregulation philosophy would pay unwelcome dividends for years to come. In November 1999, Congress repealed the Glass-Steagall Act—the culmination of a $300 million lobbying effort by the banking and financial services industries, and spearheaded in Congress by Senator Phil Gramm. Glass-Steagall had long separated commercial banks (which lend money) and investment banks (which organize the sale of bonds and equities); it had been enacted in the aftermath of the Great Depression and was meant to curb the excesses of that era, including grave conflicts of interest. For instance, without separation, if a company whose shares had been issued by an investment bank, with its strong endorsement, got into trouble, wouldn't its commercial arm, if it had one, feel pressure to lend it money, perhaps unwisely? An ensuing spiral of bad judgment is not hard to foresee. I had opposed repeal of Glass-Steagall. The proponents said, in effect, Trust us: We will create Chinese walls to make sure that the problems of the past do not recur. As an economist, I certainly possessed a healthy degree of trust, trust in the power of economic incentives to bend human behavior toward self-interest—toward short-term self-interest, at any rate, rather than Tocqueville's[3] "self-interest rightly understood."

The most important consequence of the repeal of Glass-Steagall was indirect—it lay in the way repeal changed an entire culture. Commercial banks are not supposed to be high-risk ventures; they are supposed to manage other people's money very conservatively. It is with this understanding that the government agrees to pick up the tab should they fail. Investment banks, on the other hand, have traditionally managed rich people's money—people who can take bigger risks in order to get bigger returns. When repeal of Glass-Steagall brought investment and commercial banks together, the investment bank culture came out on top. There was a demand for the kind of high returns that could be obtained only through high leverage and big risk taking.

There were other important steps down the deregulatory path. One was the decision in April 2004 by the Securities and Exchange Commission, at a meeting attended by virtually no one and largely overlooked at the time, to allow big investment banks to increase their debt-to-capital ratio (from 12:1 to 30:1, or higher) so that they could buy more mortgage-backed securities,[4] inflating the housing bubble in the process.

In agreeing to this measure, the SEC argued for the virtues of self-regulation: the peculiar notion that banks can effectively police themselves. Self-regulation is preposterous, as even Alan Greenspan now concedes, and as a practical matter it can't, in any case, identify systemic risks—the kinds of risks that arise when, for instance, the models used by each of the banks to manage their portfolios tell all the banks to sell some security all at once.

As we stripped back the old regulations, we did nothing to address the new challenges posed by 21st-century markets. The most important challenge was that posed by derivatives. In 1998 the head of the Commodity Futures Trading Commission, Brooksley Born, had called for such regulation—a concern that took on urgency after the Fed, in that same year, engineered the bailout of Long-Term Capital Management, a hedge fund whose trillion-dollar-plus failure threatened global financial markets. But Secretary of the Treasury Robert Rubin, his deputy, Larry Summers, and Greenspan were adamant—and successful—in their opposition. Nothing was done.

No. 3: Applying the Leeches

Then along came the [George W.] Bush tax cuts, enacted first on June 7, 2001, with a follow-on installment two years later. The president and his advisers seemed to believe that tax cuts, especially for upper-income Americans and corporations, were a cure-all for any economic disease—the modern-day equivalent of leeches. The tax cuts played a pivotal role in shaping the background conditions of the current crisis. Because they did very little to stimulate the economy, real stimulation was left to the Fed, which took up the task with unprecedented low interest rates and liquidity. The war in Iraq made matters worse, because it led to soaring oil prices. With America so dependent on oil imports, we had to spend several hundred billion more to purchase oil—money that otherwise would have been spent on American goods. Normally this would have led to an economic slowdown, as it had in the 1970s. But the Fed met the challenge in the most myopic way imaginable. The flood of liquidity made money readily available in mortgage markets, even to those who would normally not be able to borrow. And, yes, this succeeded in forestalling an economic downturn; America's household saving rate plummeted to zero. But it should have been clear that we were living on borrowed money and borrowed time.

The cut in the tax rate on capital gains contributed to the crisis in another way. It was a decision that turned on values: Those who speculated (read: gambled) and won were taxed more lightly than wage earners who simply worked hard. But more than that, the decision encouraged leveraging, because interest was tax-deductible. If, for instance, you borrowed a million to buy a home or took a $100,000 home equity loan to buy stock, the interest would be fully deductible every year. Any capital gains you made were taxed lightly—and at some possibly remote day in the future. The Bush administration was providing an open invitation to excessive borrowing and lending—not that American consumers needed any more encouragement.

No. 4: Faking the Numbers

Meanwhile, on July 30, 2002, in the wake of a series of major scandals—notably the collapse of WorldCom [a major telecommunications company] and Enron [a major energy company]—Congress passed the Sarbanes-Oxley Act.[5] The scandals had involved every major American accounting firm, most of our banks, and some of our premier companies, and made it clear that we had serious problems with our accounting system. Accounting is a sleep-inducing topic for most people, but if you can't have faith in a company's numbers, then you can't have faith in anything about a company at all. Unfortunately, in the negotiations over what became Sarbanes-Oxley a decision was made not to deal with what many, in-

cluding the respected former head of the SEC Arthur Levitt, believed to be a fundamental underlying problem: stock options.[6] Stock options have been defended as providing healthy incentives toward good management, but in fact they are "incentive pay" in name only. If a company does well, the CEO [chief executive officer] gets great rewards in the form of stock options; if a company does poorly, the compensation is almost as substantial but is bestowed in other ways. This is bad enough. But a collateral problem with stock options is that they provide incentives for bad accounting: Top management has every incentive to provide distorted information in order to pump up share prices.

The incentive structure of the rating agencies also proved perverse. Agencies such as Moody's and Standard & Poor's are paid by the very people they are supposed to grade. As a result, they've had every reason to give companies high ratings, in a financial version of what college professors know as grade inflation. The rating agencies, like the investment banks that were paying them, believed in financial alchemy—that F-rated toxic mortgages could be converted into products that were safe enough to be held by commercial banks and pension funds. We had seen this same failure of the rating agencies during the East Asia crisis of the 1990s: High ratings facilitated a rush of money into the region, and then a sudden reversal in the ratings brought devastation. But the financial overseers paid no attention.

No. 5: Letting It Bleed

The final turning point came with the passage of a bailout package on October 3, 2008—that is, with the administration's response to the crisis itself. We will be feeling the consequences for years to come. Both the administration and the Fed had long been driven by wishful thinking, hoping that the bad news was just a blip, and that a return to growth was just around the corner. As America's banks faced collapse, the administration veered from one course of action to another. Some institutions (Bear Stearns, AIG [American International Group], Fannie Mae, Freddie Mac) were bailed out. Lehman Brothers was not. Some shareholders got something back. Others did not.

The original proposal by Treasury Secretary Henry Paulson, a three-page document that would have provided $700 billion for the secretary to spend at his sole discretion, without oversight or judicial review, was an act of extraordinary arrogance. He sold the program as necessary to restore confidence. But it didn't address the underlying reasons for the loss of confidence. The banks had made too many bad loans. There were big holes in their balance sheets. No one knew what was truth and what was fiction. The bailout package was like a massive transfusion to a patient suffering from internal bleeding—and nothing was being done about the source of the problem, namely all those foreclosures. Valuable time was wasted as Paulson pushed his own plan, "cash for trash," buying up the bad assets and putting the risk onto American taxpayers. When he finally abandoned it, providing banks with money they needed, he did it in a way that not only cheated America's taxpayers but failed to ensure that the banks would use the money to restart lending. He even allowed the banks to pour out money to their shareholders as taxpayers were pouring money into the banks.

The other problem not addressed involved the looming weaknesses in the economy. The economy had been sustained by excessive borrowing. That game was up. As consumption contracted, exports kept the economy going, but with the dollar strengthening and Europe and the rest of the world declining, it was hard to see how that could continue. Meanwhile, states faced massive drop-offs in revenues—they would have to cut back on expenditures. Without quick action by government, the economy faced a downturn. And even if banks had lent wisely—which they hadn't—the downturn was sure to mean an increase in bad debts, further weakening the struggling financial sector.

The administration talked about confidence building, but what it delivered was actually a confidence trick. If the administration had really wanted to restore confidence in the financial system, it would have begun by addressing the underlying problems—the flawed incentive structures and the inadequate regulatory system.

Every Decision Counts

Was there any single decision which, had it been reversed, would have changed the course of history? Every decision— including decisions not to do something, as many of our bad economic decisions have been—is a consequence of prior decisions, an interlinked web stretching from the distant past into the future. You'll hear some on the Right point to certain actions by the government itself—such as the Community Reinvestment Act [CRA], which requires banks to make mortgage money available in low-income neighborhoods. (Defaults on CRA lending were actually much lower than on other lending.) There has been much finger-pointing at Fannie Mae and Freddie Mac, the two huge mortgage lenders, which were originally government-owned. But in fact they came late to the subprime[7] game, and their problem was similar to that of the private sector: Their CEOs had the same perverse incentive to indulge in gambling.

The truth is most of the individual mistakes boil down to just one: a belief that markets are self-adjusting and that the role of government should be minimal. Looking back at that belief during hearings this fall [2008] on Capitol Hill, Alan Greenspan said out loud, "I have found a flaw." Congressman Henry Waxman pushed him, responding, "In other words, you found that your view of the world, your ideology, was not right; it was not working." "Absolutely, precisely," Greenspan said. The embrace by America—and much of the rest of the world—of this flawed economic philosophy made it inevitable that we would eventually arrive at the place we are today.

Notes

1. Derivatives have no underlying financial worth but are instead financial products with worth based on changes in the value of the underlying asset. Underlying assets usually consist of stocks or groupings of stocks in an index, a specific financial event, interest rates, or commodities. Participants in derivatives are essentially wagering that the asset will either grow or decline and that they will be paid or lose their investment based on the behavior of the asset.
2. A credit default swap (CDS) is a transaction where the buyer of a bond or loan makes payments to the seller, who guarantees the creditworthiness of the product. The buyer receives a payment from the seller if the product goes into default.

3. Alexis de Tocqueville was a nineteenth-century French political thinker and historian.
4. A mortgage-backed security (MBS) represents an investor's interest in a pool of mortgage loans. These securities are created when a financial institution buys mortgages from a primary lender, sells them to various investors—spreading the risk—and uses the monthly mortgage payments to compensate investors.
5. The Sarbanes-Oxley Act was enacted in 2002 following a number of corporate and accounting scandals and set more rigorous standards for publicly traded companies.
6. Stock options offer stocks for purchase or award under favorable terms.
7. Subprime mortgages are designed for individuals with poor credit; these loan agreements are more risky than prime mortgages for lenders and more expensive for borrowers.

| "To explain the financial crisis, and avoid the next one, we should look at the failure of regulation, not at a mythical deregulation."

The Wrong Regulations, Not Deregulation, Caused the Financial Crisis

Mark A. Calabria

Mark A. Calabria is director of financial regulation studies at the Cato Institute. He served for eight years as a senior economist for the U.S. Senate Committee on Banking, Housing, and Urban Affairs.

Those who blame deregulation for the financial crisis are ignoring the fact that budget dollars supporting regulation increased during the George W. Bush administration, as did the number of regulations, Calabria argues in this viewpoint. He also disputes the assertion that the passage of the Gramm-Leach-Bliley Act, which repealed the Glass-Steagall Act and allowed commercial banks to engage in investment activities, set the stage for the crisis. Even under Glass-Steagall, commercial banks were *able to trade in many of the financial instruments at the heart of the crisis, such as derivatives. Additionally, the two notorious failures of the crisis, Bear Stearns and Lehman Brothers, were purely investment banks with no commercial banking activity, Calabria notes. The real problem, according to the author, is not deregulation, but wrongheaded regulations.*

As you read, consider the following questions:

1. The author quotes former president Bill Clinton as saying the Gramm-Leach-Bliley Act had no role in creating the financial crisis. What reasons does Clinton give for his opinion?

2. In Calabria's opinion, what is the primary flaw of a centralized counterparty?

3. What reasons does Calabria cite for his argument that greater regulation of subprime mortgages would not have prevented the crisis?

The growing narrative in Washington [D.C.] is that a decades-long unraveling of the regulatory system allowed and encouraged Wall Street to excess, resulting in the current financial crisis. Left unchallenged, this narrative will likely form the basis of any financial reform measures. Having such measures built on a flawed foundation will only ensure that future financial crises are more frequent and severe.

Rolling Back the Regulatory State?

Although it is the quality and substance of regulation that has to be the center of any debate regarding regulation's role in the financial crisis, a direct measure of regulation is the budgetary dollars and staffing levels of the financial regulatory agencies. In a Mercatus Center study, Veronique de Rugy and Melinda Warren found that outlays for banking and financial regulation increased from only $190 million in 1960 to $1.9 billion in 2000 and to more than $2.3 billion in 2008 (in constant 2000 dollars).

Focusing specifically on the Securities and Exchange Commission [SEC]—the agency at the center of Wall Street regulation—budget outlays under President George W. Bush increased in real terms by more than 76 percent, from $357 million to $629 million (2000 dollars).

However, budget dollars alone do not always translate into more cops on the beat—all those extra dollars could have been spent on the SEC's extravagant new headquarters building. In fact most of the SEC's expanded budget went into additional staff, from 2,841 full-time equivalent employees in 2000 to 3,568 in 2008, an increase of 26 percent. The SEC's 2008 staffing levels are more than eight times that of the Consumer Product Safety Commission, for example, which reviews thousands of consumer products annually.

Comparable figures for bank regulatory agencies show a slight decline from 13,310 in 2000 to 12,190 in 2008, although this is driven completely by reductions in staff at the regional Federal Reserve Banks, resulting from changes in their check-clearing activities (mostly now done electronically) and at the FDIC [Federal Deposit Insurance Corporation], as its resolution staff dealing with the bank failures of the 1990s was wound down. Other banking regulatory agencies, such as the Comptroller of the Currency—which oversees national banks like Citibank—saw significant increases in staffing levels between 2000 and 2008.

Another measure of regulation is the absolute number of rules issued by a department or agency. The primary financial regulator, the Department of the Treasury, which includes both the Office of the Comptroller of the Currency and the Office of Thrift Supervision, saw its annual average of new rules proposed increase from around 400 in the 1990s to more than 500 in the 2000s. During the 1990s and 2000s, the SEC issued about 74 rules per year.

Setting aside whether bank and securities regulators were doing their jobs aggressively or not, one thing is clear—recent years have witnessed an increasing number of regulators on the beat and an increasing number of regulations.

Gramm-Leach-Bliley Had Minimal Impact

Central to any claim that deregulation caused the crisis is the Gramm-Leach-Bliley Act. The core of Gramm-Leach-Bliley is a repeal of the New Deal–era Glass-Steagall Act's prohibition on the mixing of investment and commercial banking. Investment banks assist corporations and governments by underwriting, marketing, and advising on debt and equity issued. They often also have large trading operations where they buy and sell financial securities both on behalf of their clients and on their own account. Commercial banks accept insured deposits and make loans to households and businesses. The deregulation critique posits that once Congress cleared the way for investment and commercial banks to merge, the investment banks were given the incentive to take greater risks, while reducing the amount of equity they are required to hold against any given dollar of assets.

But there are questions about how much impact the law had on the financial markets and whether it had any influence on the current financial crisis. Even before its passage, investment banks were already allowed to trade and hold the very financial assets at the center of the financial crisis: mortgage-backed securities,[1] derivatives,[2] credit default swaps,[3] collateralized debt obligations.[4] The shift of investment banks into holding substantial trading portfolios resulted from their increased capital base as a result of most investment banks becoming publicly held companies, a structure allowed under Glass-Steagall.

Second, very few financial holding companies decided to combine investment and commercial banking activities. The two investment banks whose failures have come to symbolize

Spending Summary for the Federal Regulatory Agencies

The budget for federal regulatory agencies has continued to grow year-over-year, including under the George W. Bush administration.

	1960	1970	1980	1990
Social regulation		Millions of current dollars		
Consumer Safety and Health	$102	$222	$1,252	$1,836
Homeland Security	145	335	1,589	3,359
Transportation	42	177	550	810
Workplace	36	115	748	1,012
Environment	17	183	1,482	3,675
Energy	12	65	437	443
Total social regulation	$354	$1,097	$6,058	$11,135
Economic regulation				
Finance and banking	$40	$98	$392	$1,304
Industry-specific regulation	91	276	486	513
General business	48	113	357	727
Total economic regulation	$179	$487	$1,235	$2,544
Grand totals	$533	$1,584	$7,293	$13,679
Annualized percentage change		11.5%	16.5%	10.2%

	2000	2005	2006	2007
Social regulation		Millions of current dollars		
Consumer Safety and Health	$3,633	$5,390	$6,139	$5,830
Homeland Security	7,874	17,019	17,468	19,181
Transportation	1,476	1,954	2,360	2,437
Workplace	1,421	1,698	1,753	1,772
Environment	6,060	6,581	7,007	6,718
Energy	607	733	761	870
Total social regulation	$21,071	$33,375	$35,488	$36,809
Economic regulation				
Finance and banking	$1,965	$2,032	$2,249	$2,392
Industry-specific regulation	744	986	1,048	1,024
General business	1,674	2,887	3,027	3,306
Total economic regulation	$4,383	$5,905	$6,324	$6,722
Grand totals	$25,454	$39,280	$41,812	$43,531
Annualized percentage change	7.2%	3.8%	6.4%	4.1%

continued

		(Estimated)		% Change	
	2008	**2009**	**2010**	**2008–09**	**2009–10**

Spending Summary for the Federal Regulatory Agencies
[CONTINUED]

The budget for federal regulatory agencies has continued to grow year-over-year, including under the George W. Bush administration.

Social regulation		Millions of current dollars			
Consumer Safety and Health	$6,193	$6,883	$7,263	11.1%	5.5%
Homeland Security	21,564	25,853	26,619	19.9%	3.0%
Transportation	2,522	3,266	2,971	29.5%	−9.0%
Workplace	1,852	1,932	2,139	4.3%	10.7%
Environment	6,733	7,002	7,874	4.0%	12.4%
Energy	903	1,063	1,106	17.6%	4.0%
Total social regulation	$39,767	$45,999	$47,971	15.7%	4.3%
Economic regulation					
Finance and banking	$2,633	$2,847	$2,896	8.1%	1.7%
Industry-specific regulation	1,115	1,263	1,296	13.3%	2.6%
General business	3,467	3,507	3,681	1.1%	5.0%
Total economic regulation	$7,215	$7,616	$7,873	5.6%	3.4%
Grand totals	$46,982	$53,616	$55,844	14.1%	4.2%
Annualized percentage change	7.9%	14.1%	4.2%		

TAKEN FROM: "Spending Summary for the Federal Agencies, Selected Years," Weidenbaum Center, Washington University and Mercatus Center at George Mason University. Derived from *Budget of the United States Government* and related documents.

the financial crisis, Bear Stearns and Lehman Brothers, were not affiliated with any depository institutions. Rather, had either Bear or Lehman possessed a large source of insured deposits, they would likely have survived their short-term liquidity problems. As former president Bill Clinton told *BusinessWeek* in 2008, "I don't see that signing that bill had anything to do with the current crisis. Indeed, one of the things that has helped stabilize the current situation as much as it has is the purchase of Merrill Lynch by Bank of America, which was much smoother than it would have been if I hadn't signed that bill."

Gramm-Leach-Bliley has been presented by both its supporters and detractors as a revolution in financial services. However, the act itself had little impact on the trading activities of investment banks. The off-balance-sheet activities of Bear and Lehman were allowable prior to the act's passage. Nor did these trading activities undermine any affiliated commercial banks, as Bear and Lehman did not have affiliated commercial banks. Additionally, those large banks that did combine investment and commercial banking have survived the crisis in better shape than those that did not.

Did the SEC Deregulate Investment Banks?

One of the claimed "deregulations" resulting from the mixing of investment and commercial banking was the increase in leverage[5] by investment banks allowed by the SEC. After many investment banks became financial holding companies, European regulators moved to subject European branches of these companies to the capital regulations dictated by Basel II, a set of recommendations for bank capital regulation developed by the Basel Committee on Banking Supervision, an organization of international bank regulators. In order to protect its turf from European regulators, the SEC implemented a similar plan in 2004.

However the SEC's reduction in investment bank capital ratios was not simply a shift in existing rules. The SEC saw the rule as a movement beyond its traditional investor protection mandates to one overseeing the entire operations of an investment bank. The voluntary alternative use of Basel capital rules was viewed as only a small part of a greatly increased system of regulation, as expressed by SEC spokesman John Heine: "The commission's 2004 rule strengthened oversight of the securities markets, because prior to their adoption there was no formal regulatory oversight, no liquidity requirements, and no capital requirements for investment bank holding companies."

The enhanced requirements gave the SEC broader responsibilities in terms of the prudential supervision of investment banks and their holding companies.

Derivatives as Financial Mischief

After Gramm-Leach-Bliley, the most common claim made in support of blaming deregulation is that both Congress and regulators ignored various warnings about the risks of derivatives, particularly credit default swaps, and chose not to impose needed regulation. In 2003, [successful investor] Warren Buffett called derivatives "financial weapons of mass destruction," and warned that the concentration of derivatives risk in a few dealers posed "serious systemic problems." Buffett was not alone in calling for increased derivatives regulation.

But would additional derivatives regulation have prevented the financial crisis?

During her chairmanship of the Commodity Futures Trading Commission [CFTC] Brooksley Born published a concept paper outlining how the CFTC should approach the regulation of derivatives. Her suggestions were roundly attacked both by members of the Clinton administration, including Robert Rubin and Larry Summers, and by the leading members of the CFTC oversight committees on Capitol Hill.

Foremost among Born's suggestion was the requirement that derivatives be traded over a regulated exchange by a central counterparty, a proposal currently being pushed by Treasury secretary Timothy Geithner. Currently most derivatives are traded as individual contracts between two parties, each being a counterparty to the other, with each party bearing the risk that the other might be unable to fulfill its obligations under the contract. A central counterparty would stand between the two sides of the derivatives contract, guaranteeing the performance of each side to the other. Proponents of this approach claim a central counterpart would have prevented the concentration of derivatives risk into a few entities, such as [insurance corporation] AIG [American International Group], and would have prevented the systemic risk arising from AIG linkages with its various counterparties.

The most basic flaw in having a centralized counterparty is that it does not reduce risk at all, it simply aggregates it. It also increases the odds of a taxpayer bailout, as the government is more likely to step in and back a centralized clearinghouse than to rescue private films. In the case of AIG, Federal Reserve [the Fed] vice chairman Donald Kohn told the Senate Banking Committee that the risk to AIG's derivatives counterparties had nothing to do with the Fed's decision to bail out AIG and that all its counterparties could have withstood a default by AIG. The purpose of a centralized clearinghouse is to allow users of derivatives to separate the risk of the derivative contract from the default risk of the issuer of that contract in instances where the issuer is unable to meet its obligations. Such an arrangement would actually increase the demand and usage of derivatives.

Proponents of increased regulation of derivatives also overlook the fact that much of the use of derivatives by banks is the direct result of regulation, rather than the lack of it. To the extent that derivatives such as credit default swaps reduce the risk of loans or securities held by banks, Basel capital rules allow banks to reduce the capital held against such loans.

One of Born's proposals was to impose capital requirements on the users of derivatives. That ignores the reality that counterparties already require the posting of collateral when using derivatives. In fact, it was not the failure of its derivatives position that led to AIG's collapse but an increase in calls for greater collateral by its counterparties.

Derivatives do not create losses, they simply transfer them; for every loss on a derivative position there is a corresponding gain on the other side; losses and gains always sum to zero. The value of derivatives is that they allow the separation of various risks and the transfer of those risks to the parties best able to bear them. Transferring that risk to a centralized counterparty with capital requirements would have likely been no more effective than was aggregating the bulk of risk in our mortgages markets onto the balance sheets of Fannie Mae and Freddie Mac [government-sponsored housing enterprises]. Regulation will never be a substitute for one of the basic tenets of finance: diversification.

Regulation of Credit Rating Agencies Added to the Problem

When supposed examples of deregulation cannot be found, advocates for increased regulation often fall back on arguing that a regulator's failure to impose new regulations is proof of the harm of deregulation. The status of credit rating agencies in our financial markets is often presented as an example of such.

Credit rating agencies can potentially serve as an independent monitor of corporate behavior. That they have often failed in that role is generally agreed upon; why they've failed is the real debate. Advocates of increased regulation claim that since the rating agencies are paid by the issuers of securities,[6] their real interest is in making their clients happy by providing the highest ratings possible. In addition they claim that the rating agencies have used their "free speech" protections to avoid any legal liability or regulatory scrutiny for the content of their ratings.

The modern regulation of credit rating agencies began with the SEC's revision of its capital rules for broker-dealers in 1973. Under the SEC's capital rules, a broker-dealer must write down the value of risky or speculative securities on its balance sheet to reflect the level of risk. In defining the risk of held securities, the SEC tied the measure of risk to the credit rating of the held security, with unrated securities considered the highest risk. Bank regulators later extended this practice of outsourcing their supervision of commercial bank risk to credit rating agencies under the implementation of the Basel capital standards.

The SEC, in designing its capital rules, was concerned that, in allowing outside credit rating agencies to define risk, some rating agencies would be tempted to simply sell favorable ratings, regardless of the true risk. To solve this perceived risk, the SEC decided that only Nationally Recognized Statistical Rating Organizations [NRSROs] would have their ratings recognized by the SEC and used for complying with regulatory capital requirements. In defining the qualifications of an NRSRO, the SEC deliberately excluded new entrants and grandfathered existing firms, such as Moody's and Standard and Poor's.

In trying to address one imagined problem, a supposed race to the bottom, the SEC succeeded in creating a real problem, an entrenched oligopoly in the credit ratings industry. One result of this oligopoly is that beginning in the 1970s, rating agencies moved away from their historical practice of marketing and selling ratings largely to investors, toward selling the ratings to issuers of debt. Now that they had a captive clientele, debt issuers, the rating agencies quickly adapted their business model to this new reality.

The damage would have been large enough had the SEC stopped there. During the 1980s and 1990s, the SEC further entrenched the market control of the recognized rating agencies. For instance, in the 1980s the SEC limited money market funds to holding securities that were investment grade, as defined by the NRSROs. That requirement was later extended to money market fund holdings of commercial paper. Bank regulators and state insurance commissioners followed suit in basing their safety and soundness regulations on the use of NRSRO-approved securities.

The conflict of interest between raters and issuers is not the result of the absence of regulation; it is the direct and predictable result of regulation. The solution to this problem is to remove the NRSROs' monopoly privileges and make them compete in the marketplace.

Predatory Lending or Predatory Borrowing?

As much of the losses in the financial crisis have been concentrated in the mortgage market, and in particularly subprime mortgage–backed securities, proponents of increased regulation have argued that the financial crisis could have been avoided had federal regulators eliminated predatory mortgage practices. Such a claim ignores that the vast majority of defaulted mortgages were either held by speculators or driven by the same reasons that always drive mortgage default job loss, health care expenses, and divorce.

The mortgage characteristic most closely associated with default is the amount of borrower equity. Rather than helping to strengthen underwriting standards, the federal government has led the charge in reducing them. Over the years, the Federal Housing Administration [FHA] reduced its down payment requirements, from requiring 20 percent in the 1930s to the point today that one can get an FHA loan with only 3.5 percent down.

The predatory lending argument claims that borrowers were lured into unsustainable loans, often due to low teaser rates, which then defaulted en masse, causing declines in home values, which led to an overall decline in the housing market. For this argument to hold, the increase in the rate of foreclosure would have to precede the decline in home prices. In fact, the opposite occurred, with the national rate of home price appreciation peaking in the second quarter of 2005 and the absolute price level peaking in the second quarter of 2007; the dramatic increase in new foreclosures was not reached until the second quarter of 2007. While some feedback between prices and foreclosures is to be expected, the evidence supports the view that initial declines in price appreciation and later absolute declines in price led to increases in foreclosures rather than unsustainable loans leading to price declines.

Normally one would expect the ultimate investors in mortgage-related securities to impose market discipline on lenders, ensuring that losses stayed within expectations. Market discipline began to break down in 2005 as Fannie Mae and Freddie Mac became the largest single purchasers of subprime mortgage–backed securities. At the height of the market, Fannie and Freddie purchased over 40 percent of subprime mortgage–backed securities. These were also the same vintages that performed the worst; subprime loans originated before 2005 have performed largely within expectations. Fannie and Freddie entering this market in strength greatly increased the demand for subprime securities, and as they would ultimately be able to pass their losses onto the taxpayer, they had little incentive to effectively monitor the quality of underwriting.

Faulty Regulation Was to Blame

The past few decades have witnessed a significant expansion in the number of financial regulators and regulations, contrary to the widely held belief that our financial market regulations were "rolled back." While many regulators may have been shortsighted and overconfident in their own ability to spare our financial markets from collapse, this failing is one of regulation, not deregulation. When one scratches below the surface of the "deregulation" argument, it becomes apparent that the usual suspects, like the Gramm-Leach-Bliley Act, did not cause the current crisis and that the supposed refusal of regulators to deal with derivatives and "predatory" mortgages would have had little impact on the actual course of events, as these issues were not central to the crisis. To explain the financial crisis, and avoid the next one, we should look at the failure of regulation, not at a mythical deregulation.

Notes

1. A mortgage-backed security (MBS) represents an investor's interest in a pool of mortgage loans. These securities are created when a financial institution buys mortgages from a primary lender, sells them to various investors—spreading the risk—and uses the monthly mortgage payments to compensate investors.

2. Derivatives have no underlying financial worth but are instead financial products with worth based on changes in the value of the underlying asset. Underlying assets usually consist of stocks or groupings of stocks in an index, a specific financial event, interest rates, or commodities. Participants in derivatives are essentially wagering that the asset will either grow or decline and that they will be paid or lose their investment based on the behavior of the asset.

3. A credit default swap (CDS) is a transaction where the buyer of a bond or loan makes payments to the seller, who guarantees the creditworthiness of the product. The buyer receives a payment from the seller if the product goes into default.

4. In collateralized debt obligations (CDOs), a collection of loans or bonds are pooled together into a financial product that is then sold as a separate investment. Typically, in a CDO, one institution will make a loan and then sell the loan to another financial institution, such as an investment bank. The investment bank pools loans into financial products that are sold to investors. The original loans can be mortgages, auto loans, corporate debt, or credit card debt. The products are divided into risk categories, and investors

in the safest categories are paid off before those in the highest risk categories, as the borrowers pay off their debts.

5. Leverage is the use of debt to grow an investment.

6. A security is a financial instrument representing ownership in the issuing organization. The most common form of security is stock in a publicly traded company. Other securities include bonds, derivatives, or shares in an investment fund.

"*The prime villains behind the mess we're in were Reagan and his circle of advisers—men who forgot the lessons of America's last great financial crisis, and condemned the rest of us to repeat it.*"

Reagan-Era Deregulation Led to the Financial Crisis

Paul Krugman

Paul Krugman is a professor of economics and international affairs at Princeton University and an op-ed columnist at the New York Times. *He won the Nobel Prize in Economics in 2008. A self-described liberal, Krugman is the author or editor of more than twenty books.*

In the following viewpoint, Krugman blames the deregulatory actions put into place during the Ronald Reagan presidency for encouraging riskier behavior in the American public, thus setting the stage for the financial crisis. Fewer restrictions on mortgage lending and other consumer credit dramatically increased the level of household debt, he maintains. This level of debt made the economy vulnerable once the housing bubble burst, as people unable to afford their mortgages began default-ing on their loans, setting off a catastrophic chain reaction in the financial system.

As you read, consider the following questions:

1. What is the long-term effect of the Garn-St. Germain Depository Institutions Act that Krugman charges set the stage for the financial crisis?

2. What was the level of household debt in 1980 (when Reagan took office) and what was it in 2007?

3. Krugman names two events that took place in the late 2000s that were the direct cause of the economic crisis. What were these events?

"This bill is the most important legislation for financial institutions in the last 50 years. It provides a long-term solution for troubled thrift institutions. . . . All in all, I think we hit the jackpot." So declared Ronald Reagan in 1982, as he signed the Garn-St. Germain Depository Institutions Act.

He was, as it happened, wrong about solving the problems of the thrifts. On the contrary, the bill turned the modest-sized troubles of savings and loan [S&L] institutions into an utter catastrophe. But he was right about the legislation's significance. And as for that jackpot—well, it finally came more than 25 years later, in the form of the worst economic crisis since the Great Depression.

The Rise in Public Debt Began Under Reagan

For the more one looks into the origins of the current disaster, the clearer it becomes that the key wrong turn—the turn that made crisis inevitable—took place in the early 1980s, during the Reagan years.

Attacks on Reaganomics usually focus on rising inequality and fiscal irresponsibility. Indeed, Reagan ushered in an era in which a small minority grew vastly rich, while working families saw only meager gains. He also broke with long-standing rules of fiscal prudence.

On the latter point: Traditionally, the U.S. government ran significant budget deficits only in times of war or economic emergency. Federal debt as a percentage of GDP [gross domestic product] fell steadily from the end of World War II until 1980. But indebtedness began rising under Reagan; it fell again in the [Bill] Clinton years, but resumed its rise under the [George W.] Bush administration, leaving us ill-prepared for the emergency now upon us.

The increase in public debt was, however, dwarfed by the rise in private debt, made possible by financial deregulation. The change in America's financial rules was Reagan's biggest legacy. And it's the gift that keeps on taking.

The immediate effect of Garn-St. Germain, as I said, was to turn the thrifts from a problem into a catastrophe. The S&L crisis has been written out of the Reagan hagiography [biography that idealizes a person], but the fact is that deregulation in effect gave the industry—whose deposits were federally insured—a license to gamble with taxpayers' money, at best, or simply to loot it, at worst. By the time the government closed the books on the affair, taxpayers had lost $130 billion, back when that was a lot of money.

Private Debt Also Rose Under Reagan

But there was also a longer-term effect. Reagan-era legislative changes essentially ended [Franklin D. Roosevelt's] New Deal restrictions on mortgage lending—restrictions that, in particular, limited the ability of families to buy homes without putting a significant amount of money down.

These restrictions were put in place in the 1930s by political leaders who had just experienced a terrible financial crisis, and were trying to prevent another. But by 1980 the memory of the [Great] Depression had faded.

Regulatory Programs That Followed the Great Depression

Many of the regulatory programs started by Franklin D. Roosevelt's New Deal in the 1930s aimed to promote fairness in economic competition. That legislation required greater transparency so that investors could more intelligently judge the value of securities in the stock market. The reforms mandated a separation of commercial and investment bank activities, since speculative investments by commercial banks had been one of the principal causes of the financial crash.

Robert Brent Toplin,
"Blame Ronald Reagan for
Our Current Economic Crisis,"
LA Progressive, *September 11, 2008.*

Government, declared Reagan, is the problem, not the solution; the magic of the marketplace must be set free. And so the precautionary rules were scrapped.

Together with looser lending standards for other kinds of consumer credit, this led to a radical change in American behavior.

We weren't always a nation of big debts and low savings: In the 1970s Americans saved almost 10 percent of their income, slightly more than in the 1960s. It was only after the Reagan deregulation that thrift gradually disappeared from the American way of life, culminating in the near-zero savings rate that prevailed on the eve of the great crisis. Household debt was only 60 percent of income when Reagan took office, about the same as it was during the [John F.] Kennedy administration. By 2007 it was up to 119 percent.

All this, we were assured, was a good thing: Sure, Americans were piling up debt, and they weren't putting aside any of their income, but their finances looked fine once you took into account the rising values of their houses and their stock portfolios. Oops.

Now, the proximate causes of today's economic crisis lie in events that took place long after Reagan left office—in the global savings glut created by surpluses in China and elsewhere, and in the giant housing bubble that savings glut helped inflate.

But it was the explosion of debt over the previous quarter century that made the U.S. economy so vulnerable. Overstretched borrowers were bound to start defaulting in large numbers once the housing bubble burst and unemployment began to rise.

These defaults in turn wreaked havoc with a financial system that—also mainly thanks to Reagan-era deregulation—took on too much risk with too little capital.

There's plenty of blame to go around these days. But the prime villains behind the mess we're in were Reagan and his circle of advisers—men who forgot the lessons of America's last great financial crisis, and condemned the rest of us to repeat it.

> "The Left continues to propagate the myth that a zeal for deregulation did us in, because it prefers government interference in the marketplace."

Reagan-Era Deregulation Did Not Lead to the Financial Crisis

Stephen Spruiell

Stephen Spruiell, generally considered a conservative, is a columnist for the National Review.

In the following viewpoint, Spruiell rebuts the charges of Paul Krugman and other liberal economists that Ronald Reagan–era deregulation caused the financial crisis. Spruiell argues that regulation isn't necessary under a private enterprise system that is truly free. It wasn't deregulation that created the problem, he contends; rather, government caused the problem by failing to regulate the activities of Fannie Mae and Freddie Mac. These government-sponsored enterprises, in their misguided efforts to promote home ownership, contributed to the housing bubble by purchasing an excessive number of subprime mortgages, Spruiell concludes.

As you read, consider the following questions:

1. What evidence does Spruiell give to back his contention that government intervention, not deregulation, was responsible for the financial crisis?

2. According to Spruiell, what activities of Fannie Mae and Freddie Mac caused the mortgage market to implode?

3. What actions of the Federal Reserve contributed to the financial crisis, according to the author?

Last month [June 2009], Paul Krugman launched a campaign to pin the financial crisis on "[Ronald] Reagan and his circle of advisers." It was "Reagan-era deregulation," Krugman wrote, that led us to the "mess we're in." The substance of Krugman's screed was so tissue-thin that even ultra-liberal columnist Robert Scheer responded to it with bafflement: "How could Paul Krugman, winner of the Nobel Prize in Economics and author of generally excellent columns in the *New York Times*, get it so wrong?" So let's not credit Krugman with making a serious argument, rather than throwing a partisan grenade.

Blaming Deregulation Ignores Government's Role

The broader narrative into which Krugman's column fits, however, must be addressed. Left-wingers and Democratic partisans are united in a vigorous effort to blame deregulation for the financial crisis. Scheer, for example, agreed that deregulation set the meltdown in motion; he disagreed with Krugman only on who, specifically, was to blame. In Scheer's less partisan version of the narrative, Bill Clinton and his advisers are the "obvious villains" for having backed various deregulatory acts during the 1990s. (Of course, Republicans are hardly absent from this version of the story: Former senator

Phil Gramm is portrayed as the architect of the late-nineties deregulation that allegedly brought down the banking system.)

The argument that a lack of regulation caused the crisis is seductive in its simplicity; it completely ignores the other side of the government equation. Regulation is seldom necessary unless the discipline of a truly free market is absent—such as when the government indemnifies companies or industries against failure, or when it juices markets with generous subsidies. In the case of the housing bubble, both of these distortions were present. Wall Street titans, led by government-sponsored enterprises (GSEs) Fannie Mae and Freddie Mac, juiced like [Major League Baseball player] José Canseco until they grew "too big to fail." In retrospect, it looks like a failure to regulate; in fact, regulations wouldn't have been necessary if the government hadn't provided the steroids.

Krugman argued that the 1982 Garn-St. Germain Depository Institutions Act sowed the seeds for the 2008 financial crisis—and that, because President Reagan signed it, the blame for 2008 lies on his doorstep. Never mind that Garn-St. Germain passed by veto-proof margins in both chambers; that it was co-sponsored by prominent Democrats, including Steny Hoyer and Charles Schumer; and that it was the second of two bills that deregulated the savings and loan industry, its predecessor—the Depository Institutions Deregulation and Monetary Control Act of 1980—having been signed by President [Jimmy] Carter [a Democrat].

The line supposedly connecting Garn-St. Germain to the mortgage meltdown is itself more crooked than Lombard Street [in San Francisco]; it exists, finally, only in Krugman's imagination. For while Garn-St. Germain did pave the way for the kinds of adjustable-rate and interest-only mortgages that Wall Street gorged on during the housing boom, this result was not inevitable: Scheer points out that "as long as the banks that made those loans expected to have to carry them for 30 years, they did the due diligence needed to qualify creditworthy applicants."

What happened, according to Scheer and other subscribers to the less partisan version of the blame-deregulation narrative, is that a series of deregulatory moves in the late 1990s and early 2000s enabled the market for mortgage-backed securities[1] and other derivatives[2] to grow huge while disregarding risk. The 1999 Gramm-Leach-Bliley Act allowed depository institutions to acquire investment-banking and insurance arms. The 2000 Commodity Futures Modernization Act (CFMA) allowed derivatives (such as credit default swaps[3]) to be traded over the counter, with little regulatory oversight. And a 2004 rule change at the Securities and Exchange Commission allowed investment banks to operate with debt-to-equity ratios of over 30 to 1.

These policy changes certainly contributed to the size of the crisis, which is why the blame-deregulation narrative seems plausible at first. It is true that without Gramm-Leach-Bliley, [financial services company] Citigroup could not have grown as large as it did. But there is no evidence that Citi's size or diversity of business lines had anything to do with its overinvestment in mortgage-backed assets. Financial institutions that did not diversify made the same mistake, and they arguably fared worse during the crisis. Bear Stearns, the first investment bank to collapse under the weight of its bad assets, did not have a commercial-banking arm. Furthermore, without Gramm-Leach-Bliley, commercial bank J.P. Morgan could not have mitigated the consequences of Bear's collapse by acquiring it. (On the other hand, the Federal Reserve's facilitation of the sale of Bear created the hazardous expectation that every failed firm would get a bailout.)

As for the CFMA, [journalist] Kevin D. Williamson and I have written in these pages [*National Review*] that institutions buying credit default insurance should be required to have a real insurable interest at stake. As it stands, an institution can buy insurance on a bond it doesn't even own. That said, losses on credit default swaps have been smaller than expected, because so many transactions are "netted"—institutions buy credit protection and then sell it at a higher price, so their exposure is hedged. When [global financial services firm] Lehman Brothers declared bankruptcy, institutions that sold credit protection on Lehman bonds were projected to lose as much as $400 billion. After all the transactions cleared, though, sellers had lost only $6 billion on their Lehman trades. [Insurance corporation] AIG's [American International Group's] portfolio of credit default swaps presented a bigger problem, as the mortgage-backed assets they insured started to sour.

Government Advancement of Home Ownership Is to Blame

But, contra Scheer, deregulation was not the primary or even secondary reason that mortgage lending spun out of control. Government promotion of home ownership set the table for a massive run-up in real estate borrowing, and the Federal Reserve's loose monetary policy in the early 2000s rang the dinner bell. Add to these factors Wall Street's ability to skirt rules and influence regulators, and it is far from clear whether any amount of regulation could have quelled investors' appetite for seemingly safe mortgage debt.

By now, the case against the GSEs is well rehearsed, but it's worth restating in this context because it provides such a vivid illustration of why regulation is needed when market discipline is absent. Fannie and Freddie's role as government-chartered companies with public missions gave investors the (correct) impression that Uncle Sam would never let them fail. Thus the GSEs enjoyed borrowing costs only slightly higher than those of the federal government, and they used this subsidy to expand rapidly, doubling the amount of mortgage debt on their books every five years since 1970. (When they finally collapsed last year, they owned or guaranteed over $5 trillion in debt.)

For years, it was conservatives who argued that Fannie and Freddie had grown dangerously large and needed stronger oversight. The GSEs' old regulator, the Office of Federal Housing Enterprise Oversight, had neither the experience nor the authority to rein them in. Democrats and Republicans alike ignored these warnings, though President [George W.] Bush and the Republicans made a failed effort to reform the GSEs after a series of accounting scandals at the companies in 2003–04. (The bill died when Democratic senator Chris Dodd threatened to filibuster it.) But both parties were complicit in giving the GSEs "affordable housing" goals to meet. In 1995, the [Bill] Clinton administration lifted restrictions on the kinds of mortgages the GSEs could purchase to meet these targets; Bush increased the affordable-housing goals during his presidency.

As [scholars] Peter J. Wallison and Charles W. Calomiris pointed out in a study for the American Enterprise Institute last fall, this enabled Fannie and Freddie to purchase or secure more than $1 trillion in subprime and Alt-A loans [both risky for lenders and expensive for borrowers] between 2005 and 2007 alone. Unlike the deregulatory acts that Scheer and others are blaming, this contributed directly to the inflation of the housing bubble. Wallison and Calomiris wrote: "Without [the GSEs'] commitment to purchase the AAA tranches"[4] of the bulk of the subprime mortgage-backed securities issued between 2005 and 2007, "it is unlikely that the pools could have been formed and marketed around the world."

Investment Banks Took on Excessive Debt

To be sure, the investment banks were more than happy to buy up the rest of the toxic debt,[5] but one reason these banks took on too much leverage[6] was their confidence that, in the event of a downturn, the Fed would cut interest rates—and keep them low—to stimulate the economy. They called this "the Greenspan put" after former Fed chairman Alan

Greenspan (a "put" is a financial option purchased as protection against asset-price declines). The Fed had cut interest rates to stimulate growth after the tech bubble burst, and it had cut them to historically low levels after the 9/11 [2001 terrorist] attacks. From late 2001 to late 2004, the Fed held interest rates under 2 percent, making investors desperate for a decent rate of return. Mortgage-backed securities met that need. Harvard professor Niall Ferguson recently contended in the *New York Times* that "negative real interest rates at this time were arguably the single most important cause of the property bubble."

The Left continues to propagate the myth that a zeal for deregulation did us in, because it prefers government interference in the marketplace. That's why it's important to remember that, for the current economic disaster, government interference bears much of the blame.

Notes

1. A mortgage-backed security (MBS) represents an investor's interest in a pool of mortgage loans. These securities are created when a financial institution buys mortgages from a primary lender, sells them to various investors—spreading the risk—and uses the monthly mortgage payments to compensate investors.

2. Derivatives have no underlying financial worth but are instead financial products with worth based on changes in the value of the underlying asset. Underlying assets usually consist of stocks or groupings of stocks in an index, a specific financial event, interest rates, or commodities. Participants in derivatives are essentially wagering that the asset will either grow or decline and that they will be paid or lose their investment based on the behavior of the asset.

3. A credit default swap (CDS) is a transaction where the buyer of a bond or loan makes payments to the seller, who

guarantees the creditworthiness of the product. The buyer receives a payment from the seller if the product goes into default.

4. A tranche, the French word for slice, is one piece of a financial instrument that has its components divided into different classes. Typically, each class of tranche will be assigned a different risk value, and investors who purchase the highest-rated tranches are paid off first.

5. Toxic debts occur when an investment's assets drop in value so sharply that they are no longer saleable.

6. Leverage is the use of debt to grow an investment.

> *"Government regulations and interventions are precisely what pushed lending institutions to reduce the standards which they had traditionally required of prospective borrowers before making mortgage loans to them."*

Government Interference with the Housing Market Caused the Financial Crisis

Thomas Sowell

Thomas Sowell is an American economist, a social and political commentator, and the author of numerous books. He is a senior fellow of the Hoover Institution at Stanford University.

Many are drawing the wrong lesson from the housing crisis, claiming that deregulation caused the crisis and urging that more regulations be put in place to prevent another crisis, maintains Sowell in the following viewpoint. The answer is clearly not more government intervention, Sowell argues, since it was government interference in the housing market that was the root cause of the mortgage meltdown. Risky loans to people with bad credit were made by banks under pressure from the federal gov-

ernment to meet a goal of increasing home ownership. It was this activity, not a lack of regulation, that is to blame, contends the author.

As you read, consider the following questions:

1. What answer does Sowell give to his question—why did so many people stop making payments on their mortgages?

2. What example does the author give to support his point that sometimes the solutions that politicians create to solve a problem create a worse problem?

3. What sense of awareness does Sowell believe is crucial in evaluating policy changes?

A historian once said: "Bad ages to live through are good ages to learn from." The current economic crisis has certainly been a bad time to live through, so we can at least try to learn from it. Indeed, there are many things to *un*learn from it.

Perhaps the first thing to question is the conclusion that many seem to be deriving from today's economic debacle—namely, that more government regulation of the housing and financial markets could have prevented the housing boom and bust, with its dire repercussions, and more government regulation is the way to prevent a recurrence of today's crisis. We have seen, however, that government regulations and interventions are precisely what pushed lending institutions to reduce the standards which they had traditionally required of prospective borrowers before making mortgage loans to them. This lowering of mortgage loan standards, and the riskier loans that resulted, were crucial to the creation of a whole financial house of cards, whose collapse sent shock waves throughout the American economy, and whose repercussions have been felt internationally.

Those who are saying today that *better* regulation could lead to better results are voicing an attractive truism that is very misleading in the real world. No doubt perfect government regulation could have solved the housing market problems. But a perfect operation of the free market could have solved those problems as well. And perfect human beings could have prevented the problems from arising in the first place. But any serious attempt to deal with serious problems must begin with human beings, and human institutions, as they are—not as we wish or hope they are.

In a complex story about intricate financial arrangements, it is possible to lose sight of a plain and fundamental fact— that behind all the esoteric securities[1] and sophisticated financial dealings are simple, monthly mortgage payments from millions of home buyers across the country. When many of those payments stop coming, no amount of financial expertise in Wall Street or government regulatory intervention from Washington can save the whole investment structure built up on the foundation of those mortgage payments.

The bedrock question then is: Why did so many monthly mortgage payments stop coming? And the bedrock answer is: Because mortgage loans were made to more people whose prospects of repaying them were less than in the past. Nor was this simply a matter of misjudgment by banks and other lenders. The political pressures to meet arbitrary lending quotas, set by officials with the power of economic life and death over banks and over Fannie Mae and Freddie Mac, led to riskier lending practices than in the past.

Human beings make mistakes in both markets and government, despite the widespread notion that, when things go wrong in the market, that automatically means that the government should intervene—as if government makes no mistakes. But neither sainthood nor infallibility is the norm in Washington or in Wall Street. Any realistic assessment of the decision-making process in the market or in government must examine the incentives and constraints facing those who operate in these two venues. Above all, such an examination must be based on the hard facts about the actual consequences of decisions, regardless of the goals, hopes or rhetoric of those decisions.

Political Interventions

Government actions cannot be discussed as if government is simply the public interest personified. Government actions are political actions, and nowhere more so than in a democracy. The time horizon of elected officials is all too often bounded by the next election. Quick fixes are one result. Nor is this something new or peculiar to American politics. Writing in Britain back in 1776, Adam Smith referred to "that insidious and crafty animal, vulgarly called a statesman or politician, whose councils are directed by the momentary fluctuations of affairs."

Many of the "problems" which politicians set out to "solve," are bad consequences of previous quick-fix "solutions" created by the same politicians or by other politicians. These include housing prices in some places that take half a family's income just to put a roof over their heads. Dealing with this problem by launching nationwide housing crusades to create "affordable housing" through mortgage lending quotas and riskier lending practices tries to solve one problem by creating another. The collapse of this "solution" now confronts the country with a still bigger problem for which yet a new "solution" is being proposed, with the prospect of still bigger problems for this generation and for generations to come, who will have to pay off a national debt created by politicians who throw around the word "trillion" to the point where it has become familiar enough that its magnitude and dangers no longer evoke the alarm that they once would have. . . .

The housing market has, of course, changed drastically in the past few years, as have other things in the economy. But does all this suggest that (1) we need to change some recent bad policies or that (2) we need to restructure a whole economic system that has worked well for centuries? More specifically, does it mean that we need to allow politicians a bigger say in how American businesses are run?

Lenders did not spontaneously begin to lend to people who would not have qualified for loans under the traditional criteria that had evolved out of years of experience in the market. Such risky loans were made under growing pressures from government regulatory agencies and politicians, and even threats of prosecution from the Justice Department if the statistical profiles of borrowers whose loan applications were approved did not match the government's preconceptions.

The growth in subprime loans[2] was one way of meeting arbitrary quotas for lending to people who did not meet the criteria for loan approval that had prevailed for years. Quota lending was one of many political patches put over problems caused by previous political "solutions." Often these interventions have focused on some limited goal, with no real concern about, or even awareness of, the wider ramifications of what they were doing. It is doubtful whether most of the state politicians of the past who enacted laws to prevent branch banking had anything in mind more far-reaching than enabling local banks to avoid having to compete with branches of much bigger and better-known banks. It seems even less likely that these local politicians felt any responsibility for the thousands of bank failures during the Great Depression of the 1930s.

Nor is it likely that the national politicians of our own times, who for years made "home ownership" the touchstone of housing policy, will acknowledge any responsibility for the financial disasters and widespread unemployment today. What that means is that the voting public must at a minimum be skeptical of political spin, no matter how often it is echoed in the media. What would be even better would be to develop some sense of awareness that everything "is interconnected in the world of prices, so that the smallest change in one element is passed along the chain to millions of others." It is a caution especially apt when someone is pushing the political crusade of the day as an overriding "good thing," whether home ownership, mortgage foreclosure mitigation or a restructuring of the whole economy.

Notes

1. A security is a financial instrument representing ownership in the issuing organization. The most common form of security is stock in a publicly traded company. Other securities include bonds, derivatives, or shares in an investment fund.
2. Subprime loans are designed for individuals with poor credit; these loan agreements are more risky than prime mortgages for lenders and more expensive for borrowers.

"*The referees who were supposed to be on the field calling fouls and keeping the mortgage game fair were told to go sit on the sidelines.*"

It Was Deregulation, Not Government Intervention, That Caused the Housing Crisis

David M. Abromowitz

David M. Abromowitz is a lawyer and senior fellow at the Center for American Progress Action Fund. He is known for his work on housing policy and economic development.

In the following viewpoint, taken from a column in which Abromowitz and Daniel J. Mitchell debate who the real heroes and villains are in Congress when it comes to housing policy, Abromowitz asserts that deregulation was the culprit behind the housing crisis. Among the deregulatory activities contributing to the crisis that he cites is the failure of the Federal Reserve and the Securities and Exchange Commission to ban certain predatory mortgage company practices.

David M. Abromowitz, "Who Are the Villains of the Mortgage Mess? De-regulators Brought Us the Meltdown," www.americanprogress.org, October 14, 2008. Reproduced by permission of the author.

As you read, consider the following questions:

1. What statistics does the author cite to support his position that lending under the Community Reinvestment Act was no riskier than other mortgage lending?

2. What were some of the ways the George W. Bush administration dismantled regulations that could have prevented the mortgage crisis, according to Abromowitz?

3. What was the real way the government aided and abetted in the housing meltdown, according to the author?

[T]here is a] ... widely circulated myth that our national foreclosure crisis and "Wall Street meltdown" stem from "government intervention" that promotes affordable home ownership. Like most urban legends, this one falls apart under close examination. The real story is just the opposite—deregulation and non-intervention pulled us into the abyss.

Lending Under the Community Reinvestment Act Was Not Risky

Throughout the 1990s, federally regulated banks slowly expanded lending to low- and moderate-income families, partly due to more serious enforcement of the Community Reinvestment Act of 1977. That law simply requires that banks taking deposits from low- to moderate-income communities actually try to meet the credit needs of residents in those areas. Fannie Mae and Freddie Mac [government-sponsored housing enterprises] backed more loans to low- to moderate-income borrowers who could be responsible homeowners if allowed somewhat more flexible credit scoring and terms. The result? A strong increase in home ownership rates by the late 1990s, especially among low- to moderate-income and minority borrowers.

But these were still "prime" loans, conforming to national underwriting guidelines and income verification. Banks reserved capital for losses and were accountable for safe and sound underwriting. Not surprisingly, a careful staff review of 500 large banks in 2000 by the Federal Reserve showed that lending under the Community Reinvestment Act was neither riskier nor less profitable than other home mortgage lending.

Subprime Loans Were Mainly to Higher-Income Borrowers

Then came the explosion after 2000 in subprime loans[1] by unregulated mortgage companies. These were high-cost loans with inadequate underwriting to borrowers with poorer credit histories. By 2005–06, subprime mortgages were nearly half of all loans made to home buyers. The vast majority of these loans were to higher-income—not low- to moderate-income—borrowers.

Did government mandate this subprime surge to aid less-than-wealthy borrowers? No. And it would seem bizarre to think that the government forced Bear Stearns and other Wall Street investment banks to pocket billions in historically high profits by bundling millions of these "innovative products" into pools laxly given the highest credit ratings for sale to investors worldwide—yet many conservative commentators would have you believe this.

Deregulation of Free Markets Was to Blame

Instead, the [George W.] Bush administration and its free-market orientation, assisted by a Republican-controlled Congress advocating the same principles, systematically dismantled or under-enforced a range of rules that could have prevented the situation [from] spiraling out of control. The referees who were supposed to be on the field calling fouls and keeping the mortgage game fair were told to go sit on the sidelines. . . .

[T]his happened in many ways. Take the Federal Reserve's [the Fed's] failure in 2001, despite many warnings by consumer and other watchdog groups, to ban mortgage company

Don't Blame the Victims

Deregulation and financial market changes gave mortgage brokers the incentive to offer loans to people who couldn't afford them. . . .

Deregulation gave brokers an incentive to cheat their own standards. Let's hold them—and those that financed them—accountable, not the families and their neighbors who they misled.

Jesse Jackson, "Why Help?"
Los Angeles Sentinel, *November 1, 2007.*

practices such as charging high origination fees, providing little disclosure of the risks of adjustable interest-rate resets and retaining no risk after selling loans. This past July [2008]—seven years too late and after millions of loans had gone to foreclosure—the Fed finally invoked the Home Ownership and Equity Protection Act of 1994 and barred those "unfair, abusive or deceptive home mortgage lending practices."

Similarly, the Office of the Comptroller of the Currency in 2003 overrode efforts by states to protect their consumers from predatory mortgage lending. The Securities and Exchange Commission in 2004 permitted Wall Street investment banks—the primary creators of the loan pools now dubbed "toxic mortgage assets"[2]—to vastly increase their "leverage[3] ratio," borrow more money and lend more to mortgage brokers generating more subprime loans.

Yes, our government aided and abetted the housing market meltdown. But it did so by promoting its view of the best of what the free market could do. In many ways, the era of 2001–06 was intended to be the dress rehearsal for a pageant demonstrating that we no longer needed government involvements like Fannie Mae, Freddie Mac, the Federal Housing Administration or a regulated bank mortgage market system; the unregulated mortgage broker–Wall Street axis would do just fine, thank you. Unfortunately, we are all stuck with watching the pageant having turned into a colossal flop.

Notes

1. Subprime loans are designed for individuals with poor credit; these loan agreements are more risky than prime loans for lenders and more expensive for borrowers.
2. Toxic mortgage assets are financial investments comprised of a pool of mortgages, called mortgage-backed securities, where the overall value of the mortgaged homes in the pool drop significantly below the mortgages held on the homes. As a result, the asset decreases severely in value and is very difficult to sell.
3. Leverage is the use of debt to grow an investment.

Periodical Bibliography

The following articles have been selected to supplement the diverse views presented in this chapter.

Ralph Brauer   "Bill Clinton's Role in the Mortgage Crisis," *Progressive Historians: History for Our Future*, November 27, 2007.

Francis Fukuyama   "The Fall of America, Inc.," *Newsweek*, October 4, 2008.

James Gattuso   "Meltdowns and Myths: Did Deregulation Cause the Financial Crisis?" Heritage Foundation WebMemo, no. 2109, October 22, 2008. www.heritage.org.

Shah Gilani   "How Deregulation Eviscerated the Banking Sector Safety Net and Spawned the U.S. Financial Crisis," *Money Morning*, January 13, 2009. http://moneymorning.com.

David R. Henderson   "Are We Ailing from Too Much Deregulation?" *Cato Policy Report*, November–December 2008.

William Kleinknecht   "Happy Birthday, Ronald Reagan (Thanks for Ruining America)," AlterNet, February 6, 2009. www.alternet.org.

Provocateur   "Bank Deregulation and the Financial Meltdown," September 19, 2008.

Anthony Randazzo   "The Myth of Financial Deregulation," *Reason*, June 19, 2009.

James Ridgeway   "It's the Deregulation, Stupid," *Mother Jones*, March 27, 2008.

Lawrence H. White   "How Did We Get into This Financial Mess?" CATO Institute Briefing Paper, no. 110, November 18, 2008. www.cato.org.

CHAPTER 2

Is Greater Regulation Needed to Prevent Another Financial Crisis?

Chapter Preface

In the argument over regulation's role in preventing another financial crisis, several commentators point out that the best regulations in the world won't work in the hands of inept regulators. As Steven Pearlstein wrote in the *Washington Post* on April 15, 2009,

> Much of the existing crisis could have been prevented if the existing patchwork of agencies, using their existing powers, had simply done their jobs. Congress can create a better regulatory structure and can expand regulatory powers, but in the end, the one thing it can't legislate is the good judgment of the regulators.

History has proven the wisdom of these remarks. The savings and loan crisis of the 1980s, which resulted in the failure of 747 banks and cost U.S. taxpayers $125 billion, was termed a failure of public policy by Matthew Sherman in "A Short History of Financial Deregulation in the United States."

Sherman also points out that the regulators of the savings and loan industry simply weren't doing their jobs:

> In 1981, the Federal Home Loan Bank Board (FHLBB), the federal oversight body for the thrift industry, had approved more lax accounting standards than generally accepted, allowing thrifts to spread out recognition of losses over a ten-year period. At a time when "Reaganomics" dominated the public consciousness, regulators were urged to avoid intervention and use forbearance in private markets.... FHLBB staff in particular had a reputation as being underpaid and poorly trained, and powerful lobbyists were frequently able to delay regulation or enforcement. Some within the industry referred to the FHLBB ... as the "doormats of financial regulation."

In contrast, in establishing a regulatory framework for the financial system following the Great Depression, President

Franklin D. Roosevelt enlisted the help of several high-profile Wall Street businessmen. Perhaps his most controversial assignment was that of Joseph P. Kennedy Sr., the father of John F. Kennedy, as chairman of the newly formed Securities and Exchange Commission (SEC). One of the wealthiest men in the country at the time, Kennedy made much of his fortune on the stock market, where he occasionally engaged in practices such as insider trading[1] that would be considered illegal today. Jerome Frank, who served as chairman of the SEC from 1939–41, likened the appointment to "setting a wolf to guard a flock of sheep." Kennedy, however, is generally regarded as setting up one of the most effective regulatory agencies of the New Deal. Martin Sieff wrote in "Billionaires for U.S. Financial Reform" in the *Globalist* on February 4, 2010,

> As SEC chairman, Kennedy proved to be an outstanding success. Although he was hated by the old-line Manhattan moneymen, he succeeded in his mission. It was a case of putting an experienced crook in charge of cleaning out the crooks.

In the following chapter, as analysts and commentators debate whether more and improved financial regulation will avoid another crisis, it is instructive to remember the lesson of history—good regulators are also needed.

Note

1. Insider trading is the buying or selling of a company's stock using knowledge that is not made public and is only known to employees, board members, or others who have inside information about the company.

> "Going forward, a new regulatory re-
> gime must address the too-big-to-fail
> problem squarely."

Greater Regulation of Banking Is Needed for Economic Sustainability

Robert E. Litan

Robert E. Litan is vice president of research and policy at the Ewing Marion Kauffman Foundation, a senior fellow of economic studies at the Brookings Institution, and a member of the Pew Financial Reform Task Force.

In the following viewpoint, Litan advances five central principles for financial reform proposed by the Pew Financial Reform Task Force. The first measure is to create a financial services oversight council to monitor potential threats to financial stability. The second is to impose tighter requirements for capital on larger institutions to address the too-big-to-fail issue. The third is to create a single national financial regulator whose authority and span of control are greater than the current assortment of agencies responsible for regulation. The fourth is to impose restrictions on the derivatives market. The final principle outlined

Robert E. Litan, "Testimony of Robert E. Litan," U.S. Congress Joint Economic Committee, December 2, 2009. Reproduced by permission of the author.

by Litan is the establishment of a new federal consumer protection agency to guard against unethical and deceptive practices in the financial services industry.

As you read, consider the following questions:

1. What are some of the threats to financial stability that Litan suggests the creation of a financial services oversight council would address?

2. What regulations for large financial institutions does Litan propose to address the too-big-to-fail problem?

3. What are some of the changes to compensation policies that Litan recommends as part of regulatory reform of the derivatives market?

[T]here are some ideas and subjects already on the table that need to be addressed if we are going to put our economy on a sustainable footing. One of those subjects is fixing the financial system. Until this happens, businesses of all sizes, large and small, cannot expect to gain the credit and financing they need as long as our financial institutions remain weak and at risk of future crises. Banks won't lend otherwise, or if they do and the incentive structures that helped lead to the recent financial crisis are not fixed, we will simply embark on yet another boom-bust cycle, which none of us wants to repeat.

I understand that some feel that we should take time to better understand the causes of the financial crisis before we reform the system. While I have some sympathy with [this] view, I also believe the danger from inaction is greater. Moreover, if we remember back to the Pecora Commission that investigated the causes of the [Great] Depression, that commission only launched a debate that continues even today. Meanwhile, Congress did not hesitate then to act and, in my view, most of what it did to fix the financial system has stood the test of time remarkably well. Likewise, Congress should not wait this time to fix what clearly needs fixing. . . .

The members of the [Pew Financial Reform] Task Force extensively debated these causes and what to do about them. We ultimately did not agree on every item of reform, or agree to take up every subject that has been connected to this crisis. But we did concentrate on some of the major issues in need of legislative attention. After much very useful and instructive back and forth discussion, we agreed on some consensus recommendations, backed by what we hope is useful analysis that will help the Congress as it goes about the critical task of reforming our nation's financial laws to dramatically reduce both the likelihood and severity of future financial crises. . . .

Create a Financial Services Oversight Council

First, the U.S. must have an early warning system that prevents inappropriate and dangerous financial practices from harming the economy.

The financial crisis revealed both gaps in regulation and unanticipated interconnections among different types of financial institutions and markets. Yet no one was charged with understanding these interconnections, looking for gaps, detecting early signs of systemic threats and acting to mitigate them. The creation of a Financial Services Oversight Council (FSOC) charged with overseeing policy on systemic stability would rectify this oversight. The Fed [Federal Reserve] would carry out systemic risk monitoring and make recommendations to the FSOC, while retaining observer status on examinations of specific institutions of its choosing.

The FSOC's systemic risk policy would outline the signals of systemic threats, such as the rapid growth of credit, housing and other asset classes. The policy also would specify how and under what circumstances the responsible federal agencies should respond with measures to encourage stabilizing behavior. Such measures could include varying additions to normal standards for capital, reserves, margins, and leverage[1] (such as loan-to-value ratios for mortgages) across institutions and markets.

Increase Capital Requirements for Large Institutions

Second, no financial institution should be too big or complex to fail.

We have learned many things from this crisis, but clearly one of them is that the "well-capitalized" positions of many of our financial institutions, especially the larger ones, were an illusion. Financial institutions took on too much risk, while moving a lot of it ostensibly "off balance sheet" only to find that once the crisis hit, they had to take these "structured investment vehicles" back home, for a combination of reputational and legal reasons.

Going forward, a new regulatory regime must address the too-big-to-fail problem squarely. The Task Force believes this is best accomplished by having capital, liquidity[2] and leverage requirements rise with the size and complexity of the institution. Larger institutions that are capable of accessing the capital markets should also be required to issue a minimum amount of subordinated debt (subject to haircuts in the event of failure) that converts to equity in times of stress. In effect, this progressively tighter regulatory regime would force larger, complex institutions to have greater buffers in the event of future financial turmoil and to internalize the potential systemic risks these institutions pose to the rest of the financial institution and economy.

The Task Force also strongly endorses the notion that large institutions above a certain size maintain a "wind-up plan" approved by a single prudential financial regulator. Large, complex institutions whose plans are persistently weak should be required to divest businesses until their failure would pose significantly less risk to the financial system.

Create a National Financial Regulator

Third, one strong and smart prudential regulator should replace the current alphabet soup of agencies.

The patchwork of federal financial regulatory agencies and their jurisdictions that long pre-dated the crisis allowed regulatory capture, charter shopping, inconsistent policies, gaps in coverage, inadequate resourcing and ineffective oversight. Future arrangements must allow for the evolution of the financial system while at the same time addressing all these weaknesses. Like institutions should be subject to like regulation. As an institution changes character, there should be no regulatory barriers to corresponding changes in the manner in which it is regulated.

The Task Force believes these objectives can be best met and the problems with the current system best cured by vesting responsibility for prudential supervision and regulation in a single National Financial Regulator (NFR). The Task Force urges that no institution be pre-designated as systemically significant. The examination process must be strengthened, with more focus on risk taking and outcomes and less on process. Better recruitment, selection, training and compensation of examiners are also needed.

Regulate the Derivatives Market

Fourth, derivatives markets and market discipline broadly must be strengthened.

Derivatives[3] markets would be more secure and transparent if all over-the-counter (OTC) derivatives were recorded with trade registries, and OTC transactions were encouraged to migrate to clearinghouses and exchanges. This is best done through the judicious use of capital required for OTC derivatives that are not centrally cleared to encourage the creation and demand for standardized OTC derivatives that are easily cleared centrally and eventually traded.

Senior executives and other risk takers in financial institutions must be rewarded by compensation structures that provide incentives for constructive behavior, not imprudent risk taking. Accordingly, a significant element of such compensation should consist of very long-term restricted stock (analogous to the compensation systems in traditional financial partnerships). Prudential regulation should penalize institutions that do not maintain compensation systems that are improperly aligned with risk—for example, through higher capital requirements.

Create a Consumer Protection Agency

Finally, consumers need better protection from financial abuses.

In recent years, unethical and deceptive practices in the sale of financial products and services became an issue in the run-up to this crisis. Consumer protection was neglected even where it was mandated by statute: It was not given priority by agencies that were primarily concerned with protecting the safety and soundness of the financial institutions under their supervision.

Accordingly, the Task Force supports the creation of a new federal Consumer Protection Agency, which should have both rule-making and enforcement powers with respect to all consumer financial products currently overseen by the various federal agencies (excluding products currently regulated by the SEC [Securities and Exchange Commission] and CFTC [Commodity Futures Trading Commission] and those offered by small service providers whose financial activities are only incidental to another business).

Notes

1. Leverage is the use of debt to grow an investment.

2. Liquidity is the ability of an asset to be quickly converted to cash without affecting the asset's price.

3. Derivatives have no underlying financial worth but are instead financial products with worth based on changes in the value of the underlying asset. Underlying assets usually consist of stocks or groupings of stocks in an index, a specific financial event, interest rates, or commodities. Participants in derivatives are essentially wagering that the asset will either grow or decline and that they will be paid or lose their investment based on the behavior of the asset.

"Re-regulation could have unintended consequences, bolstering the power of well-organized interest groups, reducing access to capital and undermining America's competitive position in the huge and growing global market for financial services."

Too Much Regulation of Banking Will Impede Economic Sustainability

Robert Hahn and Peter Passell

Robert Hahn is executive director of the Reg-Markets Center and a senior fellow at the American Enterprise Institute Center for Regulatory and Market Studies. Peter Passell is a senior fellow at the Milken Institute.

In the following viewpoint, Hahn and Passell concede that the re-regulation of financial markets is an inevitable response to the mortgage meltdown. However, the wrong regulations could put the United States at a competitive disadvantage in the global financial services market. There are ample examples of mis-

Robert Hahn and Peter Passell, *The Rush to Re-Regulate*. Washington, DC: Reg-Markets Center: AEI Center for Regulatory and Market Studies, 2008. Paper was first published in the *Economist's Voice* in July 2008. Republished with permission of The Berkley Electronic Press, conveyed through Copyright Clearance Center, Inc.

guided regulations coming out of the stock market crash of 1929 that show the danger of too hasty and misguided regulations, they argue. Hahn and Passell recommend that four principles be followed in evaluating proposals for financial reform: to focus on systemic damage, to beware of fighting the last war, to emphasize the need for clear information on potential risky investments, and to make sure that the recipients of future bailouts pay a price for the public money they receive.

As you read, consider the following questions:

1. What are some examples of regulatory remedies of the 1930s that the authors deem as misguided?

2. What explanation did the President's Working Group on Financial Markets offer as the origin of the financial crisis?

3. What are some regulations coming out of the President's Working Group on Financial Markets that the authors cite as having the potential to raise costs, freeze credit markets, and reduce competition?

With Wall Street still reeling from the mortgage melt-down, the Federal Reserve [the Fed] now seemingly committed to rescuing big investment banks "too complex to fail," and the U.S. Treasury proposing a top-to-bottom reorganization of financial regulation, pieties about the virtues of unfettered markets now seem hollow. Tighter oversight of financial markets—reversing a trend that began in the 1970s with the end of fixed commissions on the U.S. stock exchanges—is thus almost certainly in the cards.

However, a little perspective is in order: Re-regulation could have unintended consequences, bolstering the power of well-organized interest groups, reducing access to capital and undermining America's competitive position in the huge and growing global market for financial services. Hence the wisdom in pausing to remember both how easy it is to fall into bad regulation—and how hard it is to dig out.

The Regulatory Rush of the 1930s

In the 1930s, the implosion of the commercial banking system and the subsequent economic depression led to a slew of remedial initiatives by Washington. Some of them helped to set the stage for recovery—think bank deposit insurance and disclosure requirements for securities[1] issuers. But much of the regulation was premised on the hoary idea that low prices were the cause rather than the effect of the economic collapse, and that the solution was the cartelization [organization into a coalition to regulate prices and output] of industries with the goal of reducing output. The broadest initiative based on that idea—the National Industrial Recovery Act, which had been championed by big businesses led by General Electric—was ruled unconstitutional in 1935. But others survived long after their faults were obvious because they benefited the incumbent interests. Agricultural price supports, underpinned by government storage programs and incentives to reduce acreage under cultivation, survived largely intact until the [Richard] Nixon administration. Trucking and airline regulation, which set prices based on petitioners' estimates of costs and assigned carriers to each route in order to prevent "destructive" competition, wasn't repealed until the late 1970s.

Today's Rush to Regulate

Politicians and regulators are now under great pressure to take names and enact reforms. Will our rush create mistakes comparable to those of the 1930s?

Probably the clearest exposition of what went wrong was offered in March [2008] by the President's Working Group on Financial Markets [PWG], the two-decades-old committee representing the Treasury, the Fed, the SEC [Securities and Exchange Commission] and the Commodity Futures Trading

Some Risk Is Not a Bad Thing

[It's] neither possible—nor desirable—to regulate away all risk. Every "bubble" is not a potential [Great] Depression. Popped bubbles and losses must occur to deter speculation and compel investors and borrowers to evaluate risk. The overregulation of finance may discourage useful innovation and clog the channels for capital on which an expanding economy depends.

Robert J. Samuelson,
"The Perils of Prosperity:
The Story Behind the Economic Crisis,"
RealClearPolitics, February 3, 2010.

Commission. The PWG diagnosed the origins of the mortgage market bust in the conflicts of interest between what economists call the "principals" (investors and home buyers) and their "agents" (mortgage brokers, securities brokers, credit analysts). Principals relied on agents to evaluate the risks on their behalf. But the agents, whose income largely depended on the number of deals they put together, had powerful incentives to understate risk. No wonder then, that principals ranging from the owners of Bear Stearns [global investment bank] stock to first-generation immigrants in California with "teaser rate" mortgages they can't refinance, were left holding the bag.

All that makes sense; the tricky part is figuring what to do about it. The PWG is inclined to connect the dots in the simplest way possible: If the agents are inherently compromised, straightjacket their ability to act in their own interests. In some cases, that would mean no more than beefing up disclosure requirements, making it harder for mortgage brokers to lead unsophisticated home buyers astray. But other regulations have the potential to raise agents' costs sharply, reduce competition and, arguably, unnecessarily pare moderate-income families' ability to borrow money and institutional investors' flexibility to manage their portfolios.

Some red flags here should be plain to all. For example, the group wants to license mortgage brokers, but who will set the hurdles that applicants must jump? In other licensed industries—everything from hairstylists to auto mechanics in many states—regulators rely heavily on the advice of incumbents, who have much to gain from keeping out competitors.

Or consider the recommendation that regulators require lenders to adjust their capital cushions to reflect their risks in falling markets. The task of measuring such risks in a world in which every major lender depends on every other major lender to honor financial contracts is truly daunting. And one must wonder whether more regulation here would drive lenders from high-risk credit on which cutting-edge businesses depend.

Principles for Regulation

We suggest evaluating reform proposals according to the following principles:

Focus on Systemic Damage. The most easily justifiable rationale for intervention is the potential for damage to those not directly involved—for example, people who lose their savings in bank runs when credit markets freeze. The Bear Stearns case confirms that public confidence is important far beyond the U.S. commercial banks that long defined the boundaries of the payments system. Today, dozens (arguably hundreds) of other large financial intermediaries are so closely tied to the payments system through counterparty arrangements in financial derivatives[2] that their failure would raise confidence questions in credit markets worldwide.

Beware Fighting the Last War. It's now clear that agents in the housing finance markets had powerful incentives to underestimate risks to be borne by others; but hindsight can be misleading in planning for the next crisis. Take, for example, the credit rating agencies' shameless inclination to bless mortgage-backed securities[3] issued by their largest customers. Won't markets correct the problem themselves, as once-burned investors treat ratings pronouncements more skeptically? Indeed, might regulation of credit raters do more harm than good by undermining investors' incentives to do their homework?

Emphasize Transparency. Housing finance markets failed because agents failed to give investors the information they needed, while home buyers and investors in mortgages didn't try very hard to get it. One would expect that this problem will largely be self-correcting, but since transparency will always be a key to efficiency in financial markets—and the sorts of information needed change rapidly as complex markets evolve—there seems much to gain and little to lose in requiring agents to provide information in forms most useful to those who bear the risks.

Public Money Should Come with Strings Attached. If the government is going to stand ready to help (the next) Bear Stearns in a pinch, the beneficiaries should pay a price. Ideally, users of funds should internalize the costs—say, by paying credit insurance premiums the way businesses pay insurance premiums for protection against fire or flood loss.

The case for doing something to prevent the next financial market meltdown is compelling. What that "something" should be, though, is not. Washington quite correctly moved quickly to shore up confidence in markets and to minimize collateral damage. However, history suggests that tackling an ambitious agenda for reform in the midst of a financial crisis is an invitation to bad regulation—regulation whose costs exceed the benefits; regulation that serves the interests of politically connected insiders rather than those of the public.

Notes

1. A security is a financial instrument representing ownership in the issuing organization. The most common form of security is stock in a publicly traded company. Other securities include bonds, derivatives, or shares in an investment fund.

2. Derivatives have no underlying financial worth but are instead financial products with worth based on changes in the value of the underlying asset. Underlying assets usually consist of stocks or groupings of stocks in an index, a specific financial event, interest rates, or commodities. Participants in derivatives are essentially wagering that the asset will either grow or decline and they they will be paid or lose their investment based on the behavior of the asset.

3. A mortgage-backed security (MBS) represents an investor's interest in a pool of mortgage loans. These securities are created when a financial institution buys mortgages from a primary lender, sells them to various investors—spreading the risk—and uses the monthly mortgage payments to compensate investors.

> *"By virtue of the combination of experi-
> ence and expertise it has developed
> ..., the Federal Reserve is well suited
> to contribute significantly to an overall
> scheme of systemic regulation."*

The Federal Reserve Should Have an Important Role in Supervision and Regulation

Ben S. Bernanke

*Ben S. Bernanke is chairman of the Board of Governors of the
U.S. Federal Reserve. He has served as director of monetary economics projects of the National Bureau of Economic Research
and as editor of* American Economic Review. *He was named
the fourth most powerful person in the world in 2008 by* Newsweek *magazine.*

*In the following viewpoint, Bernanke makes his case to the
U.S. Congress for an expanded role of the Federal Reserve Board
in banking supervision. To support his case, he points out that
many of the institutions that failed—including American International Group, Lehman Brothers, Bear Stearns, Countrywide,*

Ben S. Bernanke, "The Public Policy Case for a Role for the Federal Reserve in Bank Supervision and Regulation," Testimony of Ben Bernanke to the U.S. Senate Committee on
Banking, Housing, and Urban Affairs, pp. 2–4, 7–9, January 13, 2010. www.federal
reserve.gov.

and Washington Mutual—were outside the regulatory scope of the Federal Reserve. In addition, the activities of the shadow banking system, which includes unregulated mortgage brokers and certain financial instruments including derivatives, were also outside the Federal Reserve's supervision. The Federal Reserve's unique qualifications, Bernanke concludes, enable it to serve in the role of primary supervisor for the banking system.

As you read, consider the following questions:

1. What are the two lessons learned from the financial crisis, according to Bernanke?

2. What are some of the responsibilities of the central bank that Bernanke cites as benefiting from the Federal Reserve's supervisory role?

3. What three arguments does Bernanke advance to support his recommendation that the Federal Reserve *not* obtain the supervisory information and expertise it needs for its central bank responsibilities from other agencies?

Two important lessons learned from the current financial crisis are that all financial firms that are so large and interconnected that their failure could threaten the functioning of the financial system must be subject to strong consolidated supervision; and that supervision of financial firms must take account of systemic, or "macroprudential" risks as well as the more traditional safety-and-soundness risks affecting individual firms.

The Benefits to Effective Supervision of the Federal Reserve's Unique Expertise

Many of the large, complex, and interconnected financial firms whose collapse contributed importantly to the financial crisis avoided the more stringent consolidated supervision that is imposed on bank holding companies by the Federal Reserve. These firms—which included American International Group, Washington Mutual, Countrywide, Bear Stearns, and Lehman Brothers—were instead subject to consolidated supervision under statutory or regulatory schemes that were far less comprehensive than that applicable to bank holding companies. In addition, an unregulated shadow banking system[1] (including, for example, unregulated mortgage brokers, structured investment vehicles, other asset-backed commercial paper conduits,[2] and securities[3] lenders) had emerged that generated mortgages for distribution, funded highly rated senior tranches[4] of securitizations,[5] and engaged in maturity transformation and other financial activities outside the view of any federal supervisor.

The system for regulating bank holding companies was, in important ways, inadequate as well. One issue of concern was that the Federal Reserve's consolidated supervision of such companies was, by statute, both narrowly focused on the safety and soundness of their bank subsidiaries and heavily reliant on functional supervisors of the bank and regulated non-bank subsidiaries of these companies; in turn, the functional supervisors themselves were statutorily focused only on the safety and soundness of the specific entities they regulated. None of the federal regulators had sufficient authority to focus on the systemic risk that large banking organizations posed.

While it is clear that the framework for financial supervision must address macroprudential risks, the Federal Reserve cannot and should not be responsible for oversight of the financial system as a whole; no agency has the breadth of expertise and information needed to survey the entire system. However, by virtue of the combination of experience and expertise it has developed as consolidated supervisor of bank holding companies and state member banks and as a central bank, the Federal Reserve is well suited to contribute significantly to an overall scheme of systemic regulation, particularly in the areas of consolidated supervision and macroprudential supervision.

It is especially important that consolidated supervision address *both* safety-and-soundness risks at individual institutions and macroprudential risks. Addressing safety-and-soundness risks requires the traditional skills of bank supervisors, including expertise in examinations and off-site surveillance of complex banking organizations. The Federal Reserve has acquired and maintained that expertise as the primary supervisor of banks of all sizes, including community banks, regional banks, and large banks that are state-chartered member banks, as the consolidated supervisor of all U.S. bank holding companies, and as the supervisor of the U.S. operations of globally active foreign banks. With many non-bank financial firms having reorganized as bank holding companies during the crisis, the Federal Reserve already is quite familiar with the risk profiles of the vast majority of the large interconnected financial firms.

The Federal Reserve's Unique Expertise

Beyond traditional bank examination expertise, however, macroprudential supervision will require economic sophistication, including knowledge of the macroeconomic environment, as well as substantial expertise regarding money markets, capital markets, foreign exchange markets, and other financial markets. Expertise in these areas is essential for developing stress scenarios and identifying and addressing vulnerabilities to, and posed by, capital and other markets. The Federal Reserve has developed this expertise in the context of macroeconomic forecasting and monetary policy making. Market knowledge is acquired through daily participation in financial markets to implement monetary policy and to execute financial transactions on behalf of the U.S. Treasury and foreign governments and central banks.

Macroprudential supervision also requires extensive knowledge of payment and settlement systems to understand the interconnections between financial institutions and markets. The Federal Reserve has developed this expertise through its operation of some of the world's largest payment and settlement systems (the Fedwire funds and securities transfer systems), its supervision of key providers of payment and settlement systems (the Depository Trust Company, the CLS Bank, and the government securities clearing banks), and its long-standing leadership role in the international Committee on Payment and Settlement Systems.

The Supervisory Capital Assessment Program, or SCAP, also known as the stress test, was critical to restoring confidence in the banking system and was a watershed event for modern macroprudential supervision. The Federal Reserve, which took the lead on the SCAP, drew on its macroeconomic and markets expertise to model potential credit losses and revenues at the SCAP banks. These analyses were essential to assess the amount of capital the SCAP banks would need to absorb potential losses and continue to meet the needs of creditworthy borrowers in a more adverse economic scenario. In the future, macroprudential supervision should feature both increased use of cross-firm, horizontal exams to assess common exposures and vulnerabilities as well as forward-looking stress testing based on alternative projections for the macroeconomy.

The Benefits of the Federal Reserve's Supervisory Role

The Federal Reserve's central banking functions significantly enhance its ability to conduct its supervisory role, and offer considerable benefits for macroprudential supervision going forward. In addition, the complementarity between narrow central banking activities and supervision creates advantages in the other direction. The Federal Reserve's involvement in supervising banking institutions of a variety of sizes generates information and expertise that significantly improve the Federal Reserve's ability to effectively carry out its central bank responsibilities and that cannot be obtained reliably through other means, such as relying on reports from other supervisors. Among the central bank responsibilities that benefit from the Federal Reserve's supervisory role are crisis management, providing liquidity to depository institutions, and monetary policy. Especially since the start of the crisis in the summer of 2007, the information and expertise that the Federal Reserve has had as a result of its supervisory activities have been essential to its successful performance of these responsibilities. . . .

The Federal Reserve faces challenging decisions regarding the timing and pace of the exit from the considerable monetary accommodation put in place during the crisis. These critical policy decisions will require particularly careful assessments of developments at financial institutions and in financial markets, and their resulting implications for the real economy. For example, losses on commercial real estate loans may continue to undermine some community and regional banks and will have uneven effects across different regions of the country. At the same time, however, the improving economy may strengthen the balance sheets of other banks and conditions in many financial markets may continue to improve. Information from the supervisory process will help policy makers to assess overall credit conditions and the stability of the financial sector, and so to time appropriately the shift to reduced policy accommodation.

A natural question is whether the Federal Reserve could obtain the supervisory information and expertise it needs for its central bank responsibilities from other agencies. While it seems clear that this is possible to some extent—indeed, the Federal Reserve obtains information regarding the firms to which it lends from their primary supervisors—elimination of the Federal Reserve's role in supervision would severely undermine the Federal Reserve's ability to obtain in a timely way and to evaluate the information it needs to conduct its central banking functions effectively.

Why the Federal Reserve Should Be the Primary Supervisor

First, active involvement in supervision ensures that the Federal Reserve will have experts on its staff with significant knowledge of banking practices and financial instruments gained from the hands-on review of banking organizations and their operations, practices, activities and balance sheets. This expertise is critical to making effective use of information about financial firms and cannot be quickly created when needed. For example, without staff expertise in bank lending practices and evaluating bank asset quality, the Federal Reserve would be unable to assess independently and rapidly the condition of borrowing institutions and the value of the collateral they pledge at the discount window. This capability has been especially valuable since the Federal Reserve began providing credit at longer maturities during the crisis. Indeed, in some cases, it has been necessary for the Federal Reserve to deploy supervisory experts to provide up-to-date assessments of the condition of borrowing firms and to evaluate the collateral they were providing. Owing in part to the supervisory expertise it has been able to bring to bear in its discount window operations, the Federal Reserve has maintained its record of never bearing a loss on credit it has extended to depository institutions, despite the spike in such lending to more than $500 billion in early 2009.

Second, obtaining information from another agency would be slower and more cumbersome than obtaining it directly from financial firms. Information provided by other supervisory agencies may be stale or incomplete, particularly in a crisis, when the condition of institutions and the value of collateral can deteriorate rapidly. An independent supervisor would have its own concerns and priorities on which its supervisory staff would naturally focus, slowing the Federal Reserve's access to information in other areas. Even if the supervisory agency's staff were willing and able to provide assistance, the back-and-forth process in which the Federal Reserve must explain exactly what is needed, evaluate the information that is received, and return to the supervisor with clarifying questions and requests for additional information could slow the process appreciably.

Finally, having the legal authority to directly obtain information—through on-site examinations or otherwise—can prove critical to understanding and responding quickly to a financial crisis. While in some cases financial institutions that the Federal Reserve does not supervise may be willing to provide information to the Federal Reserve on a voluntary basis, in other cases they have not been willing, and there is no guarantee that they will be willing in future crises. For example, senior managers with relevant knowledge about the nature of the problems facing an institution or arising in financial markets may well be focused on those problems and therefore might not want to meet with, or provide information to, the Federal Reserve in a timely manner unless the Federal Reserve had the supervisory authority to require them to do so. Also, an institution may not readily recognize or acknowledge the possible adverse effects of its actions for other market participants or the financial markets and economy more generally, or it may expect the authorities to deal with such adverse effects. In such cases, it can be essential for the Federal Reserve to have the ability to compel the disrupted institution to provide timely information that would assist the Federal Reserve in addressing the crisis through its monetary policy, lending, and other policy and operational tools.

Notes

1. The shadow banking system consists of non-bank financial institutions, such as hedge funds, that act as intermediaries between investors and borrowers.
2. A conduit is a financial instrument that aggregates mortgages and other debt into a pool which is in turn sold to investors.

3. A security is a financial instrument representing ownership in the issuing organization. The most common form of security is stock in a publicly traded company. Other securities include bonds, derivatives, or shares in an investment fund.

4. A tranche, the French word for slice, is one piece of a financial instrument that has its components divided into different classes. Typically, each class of tranche will be assigned a different risk value, and investors who purchase the highest-rated tranches are paid off first.

5. Securitization is the process of aggregating similar types of investments, typically loans or mortgages, into a common pool, then selling that pool of investments.

> "As long as the [Federal Reserve] exists,
> it will regard itself as, and be regarded
> as, the economic insurer of last resort."

The Federal Reserve Should Be Eliminated

Jeffrey A. Miron

Jeffrey A. Miron is a senior lecturer and director of undergraduate studies in the Department of Economics at Harvard University and a senior fellow at the Cato Institute.

The financial crisis didn't occur because of inadequate regulation, Miron claims in the following viewpoint. Rather, it was caused by two mistaken government policies—promoting home ownership to those who were bad credit risks and bailing out institutions that failed because they took on excessive risk. The Federal Reserve was indirectly responsible for allowing each of these to occur and thus bears significant responsibility for the financial crisis, Miron contends. As long as the Federal Reserve exists, risky behavior will continue because the financial community will assume that the Federal Reserve will step in to prop up markets to prevent another financial catastrophe. This creates a moral hazard that encourages risky behavior, Miron argues.

As you read, consider the following questions:

1. What reasons does Miron give for his contention that the mortgage crisis was inevitable?

2. Miron states that the bailout of financial institutions caused much of the financial market turmoil. What evidence does he cite to support his contention?

3. Name three of the institutions Miron says should be eliminated to minimize future financial crises.

In the coming weeks and months, Congress will be turning its attention to financial market reform, in hopes of avoiding future financial crises. According to perceived wisdom, the root cause of the 2008 financial crisis was excessive risk taking, and proper regulation can detect and prevent such excess in the future.

This view is a pipe dream. Most new regulation will do nothing to limit crises because markets will innovate around it. Worse, some regulation being considered by Congress will guarantee bigger and more frequent crises.

Government-Induced Moral Hazard Caused the Crisis

The financial crisis of 2008 did not occur because of insufficient or ill-designed regulation. Rather, it resulted from two misguided government policies.

The first was the attempt to promote home ownership. Numerous policies have pursued this goal for decades, and over time, they have focused mainly on home ownership for low-income households. These policies encouraged mortgage lending to borrowers with shaky credit characteristics, such as limited income or assets, and on terms that defied common sense, such as zero down payment.

The pressure to expand risky credit was especially problematic because of the second misguided policy, the long-standing practice of bailing out failures from private risk taking. This practice meant that financial markets expected the government to cushion any losses from a crash in mortgage debt. Thus, the historical tendency to bail out creditors created an enormous moral hazard.

One crucial component of this moral hazard was the now infamous "Greenspan put," the Fed's [the Federal Reserve's] practice under Chairman Alan Greenspan of lowering interest rates in response to financial disruptions that might otherwise cause a crash in asset prices. In the early to mid-2000s, in particular, the Fed made a conscious decision not to burst the housing bubble and instead to "fix things" if a crash occurred.

It was inevitable, however, that a crash would ensue; the expansion of mortgage credit made sense only so long as housing prices kept increasing, and at some point this had to stop. Once it did, the market had no option but to unwind the positions built on untenable assumptions about housing prices. Thus government pressure to take risk, combined with implicit insurance for this risk, were the crucial causes of the bubble and the crash. Inadequate financial regulation played no significant role.

New Regulation Must Avoid Moral Hazard

If government-induced moral hazard caused the crisis, then new regulation should avoid creating or exacerbating this perverse incentive. Yet two components of proposed regulation will increase, rather than decrease, the chances for moral hazard.

One proposed change in regulation would give the Federal Reserve increased power to supervise financial institutions, especially bank holding companies such as Citigroup or Bank of America. This approach is a triumph of hope over experience. Why should an expanded Fed role be beneficial when the Fed erred so badly in the previous instance?

Defenders of an expanded Fed role will claim that, in the lead-up to the crisis, the Fed did not have explicit powers to supervise and monitor non-bank financial institutions, and that such powers could have avoided the crisis.

Yet during the years before the crisis, the Fed had more than ample power to recognize the unprecedented level of risk that was building in the economy and to issue stern warnings, whether or not it had explicit regulatory authority. In fact, far from cautioning the market to behave, the Fed promoted the notion that it could solve any problems that might result from a bursting of the housing bubble.

Regulators are fallible. Alan Greenspan, once thought to be the maestro, got it fabulously wrong. Ben Bernanke, regardless of the merits of his stewardship, will not be Fed chairman forever. Centralized and expanded power to make things better is also centralized and expanded power to make things worse. In particular, any mistakes made by a powerful, centralized authority have a magnified impact because they distort the behavior of the entire market.

Just as problematic as granting the Fed additional powers is the proposal to allow the FDIC [Federal Deposit Insurance Corporation] to resolve bank holding companies using taxpayer funds. Under the proposed arrangement, the FDIC rather than bankruptcy courts would be responsible for bank holding companies, and the FDIC would be authorized to make loans to failed institutions, to purchase their debts and other assets, to assume or guarantee their obligations, and to acquire equity interests. The funds would be borrowed from the Treasury.

This means that FDIC resolution of bank holding companies would put taxpayer skin in the game, a radical departure from standard bankruptcy and an approach that mimics the actions of the U.S. Treasury under TARP [Troubled Asset Relief Program]. Thus, the new approach would institutionalize TARP.

"Mix more punch! The US Federal Reserve has decided they want the money bowls refilled."

"Mix more punch! The US Federal Reserve has decided they want the money bowls refilled." Cartoon by Daniel Brown. www.CartoonStock.com.

The result will be that under the proposed system, bank holding companies would forever more regard themselves as explicitly, not just implicitly, backstopped by the full faith and credit of the U.S. Treasury. That is moral hazard in the extreme, and it will create an unprecedented incentive for excessive risk taking by these institutions.

The Bankruptcy Approach

The only way to limit financial panics is to eliminate government-induced moral hazard, and that means letting failed institutions fail. Whether resolution is carried out by the FDIC or a bankruptcy court is not the crucial question; rather, it is whether that resolution process forces all the losses on the institution's stakeholders rather than bailing them out with taxpayer funds.

The standard objection to allowing failures is that some financial institutions are allegedly so large or interconnected that their failure causes a breakdown of the credit mechanism, thereby harming the whole economy rather than just transmitting losses that have already occurred. According to this view, letting Lehman Brothers fail was a crucial mistake that initiated the meltdown, and bailing out other financial institutions was a necessary evil to prevent even further chaos. Nothing could be further from the truth.

Rather than being a cause, Lehman's failure was merely the signal that time had come for the U.S. economy to pay the price for all the distortions caused by the misguided policies toward housing and risk. Given those distortions, a massive unwinding and restructuring was necessary to make the economy healthy again.

This restructuring required lower residential investment, declines in stock and housing prices, and shrinkage of the financial sector. All of this implied a recession, even without any impact of financial institution failures on the credit mechanism, and the recession meant that lending would contract, even without a credit crunch.

The bailout itself, moreover, caused much of the financial market turmoil. The announcement that the Treasury was considering a bailout scared markets and froze credit because bankers did not want to realize their losses if government was going to bail them out. The bailout introduced uncertainty because no one knew what the bailout meant. The bailout did little to make balance sheets transparent, yet the market's inability to determine who was solvent was a key reason for the credit freeze.

Thus letting Lehman fail was the right decision; bailing out Bear Stearns, Fannie [Mae], and Freddie [Mac] in advance of Lehman, and the rest of Wall Street afterwards, were the mistakes. For all its warts, bankruptcy rather than bailout is the right way to resolve non-bank financial institutions. Any regulation that formalizes bailouts creates an enormous moral hazard and a black hole for taxpayer funds.

The Future

To limit future financial crises, policy must first avoid the distortions inherent in the attempt to expand home ownership. This means eliminating the Federal Housing Administration, the Federal Home Loan Banks, Fannie Mae, Freddie Mac, the Community Reinvestment Act, the deductibility of mortgage interest, the homestead exclusion in the personal bankruptcy code, the tax-favored treatment of capital gains on housing, the HOPE for Homeowners Act, the Emergency Economic Stabilization Act (the bailout bill), and the Homeowners Affordability and Stability Plan. None of this is sensible policy.

In addition, policy must end its proclivity to bail out private risk taking. This second task is difficult, since it requires policy makers to "tie their own hands." Specific changes in policies and institutions can nevertheless support this goal. The first is avoiding new regulation that makes bailouts more likely. A second is repealing all existing financial regulation, since this would signal markets that they, and only they, can truly protect themselves from risk.

The third and perhaps most important way to reduce moral hazard is to eliminate the Federal Reserve. As long as the Fed exists, it will regard itself as, and be regarded as, the economic insurer of last resort. In a world with perfect information, appropriately humble central bankers, and an absence of political influence on monetary policy, such a protector might enhance the economy's performance on average.

In the world we live in, none of these conditions will hold consistently, so the potential for policy-induced disasters is large. The U.S. economy prospered for its first 125 years without a central bank. It's time to try that approach again.

> "Curbing the proprietary interests of commercial banks is in the interest of fair and open competition as well as protecting the provision of essential financial services."

The Obama Administration's Regulatory Reform Will Reduce Risk in Banking

Paul A. Volcker

Paul A. Volcker, an economist, was chairman of the Federal Reserve Board from 1979 to 1987. He is currently chairman of President Barack Obama's Economic Recovery Advisory Board.

In the following viewpoint, taken from his testimony before the U.S. Senate Committee on Banking, Housing, and Urban Affairs, Volcker recommends that risk be diminished in financial markets by prohibiting commercial banks from engaging in proprietary and speculative trading. Commercial banks quite appropriately have a government safety net protecting consumers if the banks falter. However, it is not appropriate to use taxpayer funds

Paul A. Volcker, "Statement of Paul A. Volcker before the Committee on Banking, Housing, and Urban Affairs of the United States Senate," pp. 1–5, February 2, 2010. http:// banking.senate.gov.

to bail out banks that are engaging in speculative trading activity, Volcker argues, and thus these investment activities should be separated from commercial banking.

As you read, consider the following questions:

1. What regulatory measures does Volcker believe are needed to minimize failure within more speculative financial institutions?

2. What path does the author think should be followed for speculative financial institutions that fail?

3. What reasons does Volcker give to support his opinion that it is a conflict of interest for commercial banks to engage in proprietary investment?

You [the Senate Committee on Banking, Housing, and Urban Affairs] have an important responsibility in considering and acting upon a range of issues relevant to needed reform of the financial system. That system, as you well know, broke down under pressure, posing unacceptable risks for an economy already in recession. I appreciate the opportunity today to discuss with you one key element in the reform effort that President [Barack] Obama set out so forcibly a few days ago [in early 2010].

That proposal, if enacted, would restrict commercial banking organizations from certain proprietary and more speculative activities. In itself, that would be a significant measure to reduce risk. However, the first point I want to emphasize is that the proposed restrictions should be understood as a part of the broader effort for structural reform. It is particularly designed to help deal with the problem of "too big to fail" and the related moral hazard that looms so large as an aftermath of the emergency rescues of financial institutions, bank and non-bank, in the midst of crises. . . .

A Safety Net Is Not Appropriate for Speculative Banking

The basic point is that there has been, and remains, a strong public interest in providing a "safety net"—in particular, deposit insurance and the provision of liquidity[1] in emergencies—for commercial banks carrying out essential services. There is not, however, a similar rationale for public funds—taxpayer funds—protecting and supporting essentially proprietary and speculative activities. Hedge funds[2], private equity funds[3], and trading activities unrelated to customer needs and continuing banking relationships should stand on their own, without the subsidies implied by public support for depository institutions.

Those quintessential capital market activities have become part of the natural realm of investment banks. A number of the most prominent of those firms, each heavily engaged in trading and other proprietary activity, failed or were forced into publicly assisted mergers under the pressure of the crisis. It also became necessary to provide public support via the Federal Reserve, the Federal Deposit Insurance Corporation, or the Treasury to the largest remaining American investment banks, both of which assumed the cloak of a banking license to facilitate the assistance. The world's largest insurance company, caught up in a huge portfolio of credit default swaps quite apart from its basic business, was rescued only by the injection of many tens of billions of dollars of public loans and equity capital. Not so incidentally, the huge financial affiliate of one of our largest industrial companies was also extended the privilege of a banking license and granted large assistance contrary to long-standing public policy against combinations of banking and commerce.

What we plainly need are authority and methods to minimize the occurrence of those failures that threaten the basic fabric of financial markets. The first line of defense, along the lines of administration proposals and the provisions in the

[Financial Regulatory Reform] Bill passed by the House last year [2009], must be authority to regulate certain characteristics of systemically important non-bank financial institutions. The essential need is to guard against excessive leverage[4] and to insist upon adequate capital and liquidity.

It is critically important that those institutions, its managers and its creditors, do not assume a public rescue will be forthcoming in time of pressure. To make that credible, there is a clear need for a new "resolution authority," an approach recommended by the administration last year and included in the House bill. The concept is widely supported internationally. The idea is that, with procedural safeguards, a designated agency be provided authority to intervene and take control of a major financial institution on the brink of failure. The mandate is to arrange an orderly liquidation or merger. In other words, euthanasia not a rescue.

Apart from the very limited number of such "systemically significant" non-bank institutions, there are literally thousands of hedge funds, private equity funds, and other private financial institutions actively competing in the capital markets. They are typically financed with substantial equity provided by their partners or by other sophisticated investors. They are, and should be, free to trade, to innovate, to invest—and to fail. Managements, stockholders or partners would be at risk, able to profit handsomely or to fail entirely, as appropriate in a competitive free enterprise system.

Now, I want to deal as specifically as I can with questions that have arisen about the president's recent proposal.

Making Appropriate Distinctions Would Not Be Difficult

First, surely a strong international consensus on the proposed approach would be appropriate, particularly across those few nations hosting large multinational banks and active financial markets. The needed consensus remains to be tested. However,

The President's New Limits on Banks

Banks will no longer be allowed to own, invest, or sponsor hedge funds, private equity funds, or proprietary trading operations for their own profit, unrelated to serving their customers. If financial firms want to trade for profit, that's something they're free to do.... But these firms should not be allowed to run these hedge funds and private equity funds while running a bank backed by the American people.

Barack Obama,
"Remarks by the President on Financial Reform,"
January 21, 2010.

judging from what we know and read about the attitude of a number of responsible officials and commentators, I believe there are substantial grounds to anticipate success as the approach is fully understood.

Second, the functional definition of hedge funds and private equity funds that commercial banks would be forbidden to own or sponsor is not difficult. As with any new regulatory approach, authority provided to the appropriate supervisory agency should be carefully specified. It also needs to be broad enough to encompass efforts sure to come to circumvent the intent of the law. We do not need or want a new breed of bank-based funds that in all but name would function as hedge or equity funds.

Similarly, every banker I speak with knows very well what "proprietary trading" means and implies. My understanding is that only a handful of large commercial banks—maybe four or five in the United States and perhaps a couple of dozen worldwide—are now engaged in this activity in volume. In the past, they have sometimes explicitly labeled a trading affiliate or division as "proprietary," with the connotation that the activity is, or should be, insulated from customer relations.

Most of those institutions and many others are engaged in meeting customer needs to buy or sell securities: stocks or bonds, derivatives, various commodities or other investments. Those activities may involve taking temporary positions. In the process, there will be temptations to speculate by aggressive, highly remunerated traders.

Balancing Banks' and Customers' Interests

Given strong legislative direction, bank supervisors should be able to appraise the nature of those trading activities and contain excesses. An analysis of volume relative to customer relationships and of the relative volatility of gains and losses would go a long way toward informing such judgments. For instance, patterns of exceptionally large gains and losses over a period of time in the "trading book" should raise an examiner's eyebrows. Persisting over time, the result should be not just raised eyebrows but substantially raised capital requirements.

Third, I want to note the strong conflicts of interest inherent in the participation of commercial banking organizations in proprietary or private investment activity. That is especially evident for banks conducting substantial investment management activities, in which they are acting explicitly or implicitly in a fiduciary capacity. When the bank itself is a "customer," i.e., it is trading for its own account, it will almost inevitably find itself, consciously or inadvertently, acting at cross purposes to the interests of an unrelated commercial customer of a bank. "Inside" hedge funds and equity funds with outside partners may generate generous fees for the bank without the test of market pricing, and those same "inside" funds may be favored over outside competition in placing funds for clients. More generally, proprietary trading activity should not be able to profit from knowledge of customer trades.

I am not so naïve as to think that all potential conflicts can or should be expunged from banking or other businesses. But neither am I so naïve as to think that, even with the best efforts of boards and management, so-called Chinese walls can remain impermeable against the pressures to seek maximum profit and personal remuneration.

Commercial Banks Will Retain Many Vital Functions

In concluding, it may be useful to remind you of the wide range of potentially profitable services that are within the province of commercial banks.

- First of all, basic payments services, local, national and worldwide, ranging from the now ubiquitous automatic teller machines to highly sophisticated cash balance management;

- Safe and liquid depository facilities, including especially deposits contractually payable on demand;

- Credit for individuals, governments and businesses, large and small, including credit guarantees and originating and securitizing mortgages or other credits under appropriate conditions;

- Analogous to commercial lending, underwriting of corporate and government securities, with related market making;

- Brokerage accounts for individuals and businesses, including "prime brokerage" for independent hedge and equity funds;

- Investment management and investment advisory services, including "Funds of Funds" providing customers with access to independent hedge or equity funds;

- Trust and estate planning and administration;

- Custody and safekeeping arrangements for securities and valuables.

Quite a list. More than enough, I submit to you, to provide the base for strong, competitive—and profitable—commercial banking organizations, able to stand on their own feet domestically and internationally in fair times and foul.

What we can do, what we should do, is recognize that curbing the proprietary interests of commercial banks is in the interest of fair and open competition as well as protecting the provision of essential financial services. Recurrent pressures, volatility and uncertainties are inherent in our market-oriented, profit-seeking financial system. By appropriately defining the business of commercial banks, and by providing for the complementary resolution authority to deal with an impending failure of very large capital market institutions, we can go a long way toward promoting the combination of competition, innovation, and underlying stability that we seek.

Notes

1. Liquidity is the ability of an asset to be quickly converted to cash without affecting the asset's price.
2. A hedge fund is a private investment pool characterized by unconventional investment methods and minimal regulation. These funds typically undertake balanced risks to ensure profit regardless of market conditions.
3. Private equity funds are pools of investments from institutions and wealthy individuals into capital used to purchase or invest in companies. Private equity firms are typically limited partnerships; thus the companies they purchase are considered privately held and are not traded on the stock market. Most private equity funds are used to purchase companies that the investors believe can be restructured

and eventually either resold or returned to the stock market through a leveraged buyout at a profit to the private equity firm.

4. Leverage is the use of debt to grow an investment.

> *"While numerical limits and strict rules may sound simple, there is great potential that they would undermine the goals of economic stability, growth, and job creation that policy makers are trying to promote."*

The Obama Administration's Regulatory Reform Will Not Reduce Risk in Banking

Barry Zubrow

Barry Zubrow is chief risk officer and executive vice president of JPMorgan Chase & Co.

Preventing commercial banks from engaging in proprietary trading won't address the causes of the financial crisis and will make U.S. banks less competitive in the global market, Zubrow argues in the following viewpoint, taken from his testimony before the U.S. Senate Committee on Banking, Housing, and Urban Affairs. It was not the investment activities of banks that led to their failure; it was their traditional mortgage business. Restricting proprietary trading could actually increase risk and make it more difficult for businesses to secure credit, Zubrow

"Testimony of Barry Zubrow," banking.senate.gov, February 4, 2010. Reproduced by permission of Barry Zubrow.

contends. Meaningful financial reform should take the form of modernizing regulations to reflect the complexities of the current financial services market, the author maintains, and giving regulators the authority and resources they need to effectively do their jobs.

As you read, consider the following questions:

1. Why does Zubrow suggest that all systemically important institutions must be accountable to the same standards?

2. According to the author, why might foreign banks gain a competitive advantage in the wake of regulation?

3. What are some of the negative consequences that Zubrow predicts could happen under the Obama administration's proposal to place a cap on liabilities?

Two weeks ago [in January 2010], the [Barack Obama] administration proposed new restrictions on financial firms. The first would prohibit banks from "owning, investing in or sponsoring a hedge fund[1] or a private equity fund[2], or proprietary trading operations" that are not related to serving customers. The new proposals are a divergence from the hard work being done by legislators, central banks and regulators around the world to address the root causes of the financial crisis and establish robust mechanisms to properly regulate systemically important financial institutions.

Restrictions on Proprietary Trading and Bank Ownership of Private Equity and Hedge Funds

While there may be valid reasons to examine these activities, there should be no misunderstanding: The activities the administration proposes to restrict did not cause the financial crisis. In no case were bank-held deposits threatened by any of these activities. Indeed, in many cases, those activities diversified financial institutions' revenue streams and served as a source of stability. The firms that failed did so largely as a result of traditional lending and real estate–related activities. The failures of Wachovia [Corporation], Washington Mutual, Countrywide, and IndyMac [Mortgage Services] were due to defaulting subprime mortgages[3]. Bear Stearns, Lehman [Brothers], and Merrill Lynch were all damaged by their excessive exposure to real estate credit risk.

Further, regulators currently have the authority to ensure that risks are adequately managed in the areas the administration proposes to restrict. Regulators and capital standards–setting bodies are empowered, and must utilize those powers, to ensure that financial companies of all types are appropriately capitalized at the holding company level (as we are at JPMorgan Chase [JPMC]).

While bank holding companies may engage in proprietary trading and own hedge funds or private equity firms, comprehensive rules are in place that severely restrict the extent to which insured deposits may finance these activities. And regulators have the authority to examine all of these activities. Indeed, existing U.S. rules require that firms increase the amount of capital they hold as their private equity investments increase as a percentage of capital, effectively restraining their private equity portfolios.

While regulators have the tools they need to address these activities in bank holding companies, we need to take the next logical step of extending these authorities to all systemically important firms regardless of their legal structure. If the last two years have taught us anything, it is that threats to our financial system can and do originate in non-depository institutions. Thus, any new regulatory framework should reach all systemically important entities—including investment banks—whether or not they have insured deposit-based business; all systemically important institutions should be regulated to the same rigorous standard. If we leave outside the scope of rigorous regulation those institutions that are interconnected and integral to the provision of credit, capital and liquidity in our system, we will be right back where we were before this crisis began. We will return to the same regime in which Bear Stearns and Lehman Brothers both failed and other systemically important institutions nearly brought the system to its knees. We cannot have two tiers of regulation for systemically important firms.

The Backlash from Federal Restrictions

As I noted at the outset, it is also very important that we get the details right. Thus far, the administration has offered few details on what is meant by "proprietary trading." Some traditional bank holding company activities, including real estate and corporate lending, expose these companies to risks that have to be managed by trading desks. Any individual trade, taken in isolation, might appear to be "proprietary trading," but in fact is part of the mosaic of serving clients and properly managing the firm's risks. Restricting activities that could loosely be defined as proprietary trading would reduce the safety and soundness of our banking institutions, raise the cost of capital formation, and restrict the availability of credit for businesses, large and small—with no commensurate benefit in reduced systemic risk.

Similarly, the administration has yet to define "ownership or sponsorship" of hedge fund and private equity activities. Asset managers, including JPMorgan Chase, serve a broad range of clients, including individuals, universities, and pensions, and need to offer these investors a broad range of investment opportunities in all types of asset classes. In each case, investments are designed to meet the specific needs of the client.

Our capital markets rely upon diversified financial firms equipped to meet a wide range of financing needs for companies of all sizes and at all stages of maturity, and the manner in which these firms are provided financing is continually evolving in response to market demand. Codifying strict statutory rules about which firms can participate will distort the market for these services—and result in more and more activities taking place outside the scope of regulatory scrutiny. Rather, Congress should mandate strong capital and liquidity[4] standards, give regulators the authority they need to supervise these firms and activities, and conduct rigorous oversight to ensure accountability.

While we agree that the United States must show leadership in regulating financial firms, if we take an approach that is out of sync with other major countries around the world without demonstrable risk-reduction benefits, we will dramatically weaken our financial institutions' ability to be competitive and serve the needs of our clients. Asset management firms (including hedge funds and private investment firms) play a very important role in today's capital markets, helping to allocate capital between providers and users. The concept of arbitrarily separating different elements of the capital formation process appears to be under consideration only in the U.S. Forcing our most competitive financial firms to divest themselves of these business lines will make them less competitive globally, allowing foreign firms to step in to attract the capital and talent now involved in these activities. Foreign banks will gain when U.S. banks cede the field.

Concentration Limits

The second of the recent administration proposals would limit the size of financial firms by "growth in market share of liabilities." Again, while the administration has not provided much detail, the proposal appears to be based on the assumption that the size of financial firms or concentration within the financial sector contributed to the crisis.

Proprietary Trading Didn't Contribute to the Crisis

Bank holding companies, . . . because they are not banks and not government-backed, can engage in any financial activity, including securities dealing. Why would we prohibit them from doing so when they are using their own funds? . . .

Mr. [Barack] Obama is arguing that bank holding companies should be prohibited from proprietary trading because it's too risky. The trouble is that proprietary trading is a profitable business . . . , and there is no evidence that it caused serious losses for either banks or bank holding companies.

Peter J. Wallison,
"The President's Bank Reforms Don't Add Up,"
Wall Street Journal, *January 25, 2010.*

If you consider the institutions that failed during the crisis, some of the largest and most consequential failures were stand-alone investment banks, mortgage companies, thrifts, and insurance companies—not the diversified financial firms that presumably are the target of this proposal. It was not AIG's [American International Group's] and Bear Stearns's size but their interconnection to other firms that prompted the government to step in. In fact, JPMC's capabilities, size, and diversity were essential to our withstanding the crisis and emerging as a stronger firm—and put us in a position to acquire Bear Stearns and Washington Mutual when the government asked us to. Had we not been able to purchase these companies, the crisis would have been far worse.

With regard to concentration specifically, it is important to note that the U.S. financial system is much less concentrated than the systems of most other developed nations. Our system is the 2nd least concentrated among OECD [Organisation for Economic Co-operation and Development] countries, just behind Luxembourg; the top 3 banks in the U.S. held 34% of banking assets in 2007 vs. an average for the rest of the OECD of 69%.

An artificial cap on liabilities will likely have significant negative consequences. For the most part, banks' liabilities and capital support the asset growth of its loan and lending activities. By artificially capping liabilities, banks may be incented to reduce the growth of assets or the size of their existing balance sheet, which in turn would restrict their ability to make loans to consumers and businesses, as well as to invest in government debt. Capping the scale and scope of healthy financial firms cedes competitive ground to foreign firms and to less regulated, non-bank financial firms—which will make it more difficult for regulators to monitor systemic risk. It would likely come at the expense of economic growth at home. No other country in the world has a Glass-Steagall regime [referring to a 1933 law to reform banks and control speculation] or the constraints recently proposed by the administration, nor does any country appear interested in adopting one. International bodies have long declined to embrace such constraints as an approach to regulatory reform.

Overly Strict Regulation Will Hamper Economic Growth

We have consistently endorsed the need for meaningful regulatory reform and have worked hard to provide the Committee and others with information and data to advance such reform. We agree that it is critically important to eliminate any implicit financial "safety net" by assuring appropriate capital standards, risk management and regulatory oversight on a consistent and cohesive basis for all financial firms, and, ultimately, having a robust regime that allows any firm to fail if it is mismanaged.

While numerical limits and strict rules may sound simple, there is great potential that they would undermine the goals of economic stability, growth, and job creation that policy makers are trying to promote. The better solution is modernization of our financial regulatory regime that gives regulators the authority and resources they need to do the rigorous oversight involved in examining a firm's balance sheet and lending practices. Effective examination allows regulators to understand the risks institutions are taking and how those risks are likely to change under different economic scenarios.

It is vital that policy makers and those with a stake in our financial system work together to overhaul our regulatory structure thoughtfully and well. Clearly, such work needs to be done in harmony with other countries around the world. While the specific changes required by reform may seem arcane and technical, they are critical to the future of our whole economy. We look forward to working with the Committee to enact the reforms that will position our financial industry and economy as a whole for sustained growth for decades to come.

Notes

1. A hedge fund is a private investment pool characterized by unconventional investment methods and minimal regulation. These funds typically undertake balanced risks to ensure profit regardless of market conditions.
2. Private equity funds are pools of investments from institutions and wealthy individuals into capital used to purchase or invest in companies. Private equity firms are typically limited partnerships; thus the companies they purchase are considered privately held and are not traded on the stock market. Most private equity funds are used to purchase companies that the investors believe can be restructured and eventually either resold or returned to the stock market through a leveraged buyout at a profit to the private equity firm.

3. Subprime mortgages are designed for individuals with poor credit; these loan agreements are more risky than prime mortgages for lenders and more expensive for borrowers.
4. Liquidity is the ability of an asset to be quickly converted to cash without affecting the asset's price.

Periodical Bibliography

The following articles have been selected to supplement the diverse views presented in this chapter.

David M. Herszenhorn "Senate Republicans Call Reform Bill a 'Takeover' of the Banking Industry," *New York Times*, May 18, 2010.

Arianna Huffington "Wall Street, DC, and the New Financial Euphoria," *Huffington Post*, May 11, 2009.

David C. John "The Obama Financial Regulatory Reform Plan: Poor Policy and Missed Opportunities," Heritage Foundation WebMemo, no. 2545, July 15, 2009. www.heritage.org.

Ezra Klein "Wall Street Reform vs. Financial Regulation Reform," *Washington Post*, April 13, 2010.

Robert Lenzner "Financial Regulatory Reform Isn't Happening," *Forbes*, February 9, 2010.

Jim Manzi "President Obama's Excellent New Banking Proposal," *National Review Online*, January 21, 2010. www.nationalreview.com.

Steven Pearlstein "Reinventing Regulation," *Washington Post*, April 15, 2009.

Harvey L. Pitt "Learning from History on Financial Reform," *Wall Street Journal*, May 17, 2010.

Nomi Prins "Obama's Half-Baked Bank Reform," *Daily Beast*, January 21, 2010.

Charles Wyplosz "The ICMB-CEPR Geneva Report: 'The Future of Financial Regulation,'" VoxEU.org, January 27, 2009. www.voxeu.org.

CHAPTER 3

Should Certain Industries Be Deregulated?

Chapter Preface

In the years from 1970 to 2000, deregulation occurred in a number of industries, prompted by the theory that a competitive environment would result in economic growth with better service at lower costs for consumers. Airlines, telecommunications, trucking, energy, and banking were some of the industries deregulated during this period. While opinions differ in each of these industries about whether deregulation delivered on its promises, one thing is clear: Some companies flourished in a deregulatory environment, and others failed. There are lessons to be learned from the actions of successful companies and those of failed companies, and those lessons can be applied to other industries in transition.

One very powerful example exists in the airline industry. Airline deregulation occurred in 1978. Prior to deregulation, Southwest Airlines was a Dallas-based niche player in the industry, with market share of less than 1 percent. In 1978, Braniff International Airways was one of the fastest-growing and most profitable airlines in the United States. By 1982, Braniff filed for bankruptcy, the first of a number of airline failures attributable to deregulation. In contrast, Southwest began a rapid growth trajectory that made it in 2009 the largest airline in the world in terms of numbers of passengers flown as well as one of the most profitable. What did Southwest do right, and what did Braniff do wrong?

According to Jonathan Byrnes, in "Airline Deregulation: Lessons for Telecom," written for the Harvard Business School, the difference was the strategy each chose to follow:

> Deregulation pervasively changed the airline industry's underlying economic structure, necessitating a fundamental redirection of each airline's strategy. The key determinant of success or failure was whether a carrier reset its strategic paradigm—its underlying set of assumptions about the

industry's economic structure and the basic competitive "win" strategies. Successful carriers comprehensively redirected their strategies to rest upon the industry's new bases for enduring advantage.

Executives at Braniff believed that the key to success in a deregulated environment was dependent on size. They quickly executed what was then the greatest expansion in airline history, expanding their domestic routes by 50 percent and adding international routes. The cost of new terminals, new aircraft, and a payroll increase of 25 percent raised the company's long-term debt by more than $305 million from 1978 to the end of 1979. Operations on these new routes began with little marketing and insufficient training of new personnel. As a result, the new customer base failed to materialize. Faced with huge debt and insufficient cash flow, Braniff filed for bankruptcy in 1989 and ceased operations in 1990.

Southwest developed a low-cost business model. By keeping operational costs at the lowest level in the industry, and by using only one type of aircraft, a policy that would reduce the number of planes sitting idly, Southwest was able to successfully enter new markets as the low-cost provider. In another effort to contain costs, Southwest uses where possible secondary airports, where operational costs are fewer. Examples are Love Field in Dallas and Chicago Midway International Airport. Additionally, instead of using the "hub-and-spoke" flight routing system of most other airlines, Southwest adopted a "point-to-point" system. Only 20 percent of Southwest passengers connect to another flight—a significantly lower figure than most airlines. Since more flight segments per passenger are a greater expense for the airline, Southwest's concentration on very dense, short-haul markets is another way in which it improves its profitability. A term, "the Southwest Effect," has been coined to describe what happens when Southwest enters a new market: Prices drop, as competitors try to match Southwest's low fares. Air travel increases, as consumers take advantage of these lower fares. And Southwest historically prevails against its competitors in a price war, since it has the lowest cost structure.

In the chapter that follows, analysts and commentators examine the pros and cons of deregulation in several industries.

"The question . . . isn't why more carriers haven't thrived under deregulation, it's why so many inefficient ones have survived for so long."

Deregulation Has Helped the Airline Industry

Loren Steffy

Loren Steffy is the business columnist for the Houston Chronicle.

In the following viewpoint, Steffy points to the success of Southwest Airlines to support his contention that deregulation is a good thing for airlines that are well managed. Southwest has grown and thrived financially in a deregulated environment, keeping fares low and enabling more people to fly. Other airlines blame the competitive environment of deregulation for their ills, when the real issue is a lack of efficiency, Steffy suggests.

As you read, consider the following questions:

1. What is one measure Bob Crandall recommends for re-regulating the airline industry?

2. What role has the rising price of fuel played in the hub-and-spoke route system?

3. How has Southwest Airlines added to its competitive advantage over its rivals?

Thirty years later, we still can't decide.

Was airline deregulation good? The answer depends on whom you ask. Last week [in June 2008], I asked Herb Kelleher, the co-founder of Southwest Airlines who retired as chairman last month.

Different Perspectives

Southwest is the only child of deregulation to reach adulthood. It's poised to surpass Northwest [Airlines] as the fifth-largest U.S. airline by traffic, according to Bloomberg News.

As its co-founder, Kelleher is the only executive who's figured out not only how to make competition work, but how to thrive on it.

To Kelleher, the answer to the deregulation question is obvious. More people can fly today for less money, even with the recent fare hikes.

"It was a tremendous boon for the 85 percent of Americans that had not been able to fly prior to deregulation," he told me last week. "Flying is still a heck of a bargain. In constant dollars, fares are still lower than they were prior to deregulation."

Just days after Kelleher told me that, his friend and old rival Bob Crandall, the retired chairman of American Airlines, gave a speech in which he called, essentially, for re-regulating the industry.

"We have failed to confront the reality that unfettered competition just doesn't work very well in certain industries, as amply demonstrated by our airline experience," Crandall said, according to a transcript.

Even though he opposed deregulation 30 years ago, Crandall helped define it. He invented the frequent flyer program,

Partial Deregulation Has Produced Benefits

Even the partial freeing of the air travel sector has had overwhelmingly positive results. Air travel has dramatically increased and prices have fallen. After deregulation, airlines reconfigured their routes and equipment, making possible improvements in capacity utilization. These efficiency effects democratized air travel, making it more accessible to the general public.

Fred L. Smith Jr. and Braden Cox,
"Airline Deregulation,"
The Concise Encyclopedia of Economics, *2008.*

and he turned the hub-and-spoke route system into the industry standard. His cost-cutting efforts—such as removing olives from salads—are almost as legendary as Kelleher's.

Both men view deregulation differently because they see it through vastly different carriers. One works, the other doesn't.

Most big airlines like American are being battered by the latest downturn in aviation, just another gyration in a boombust undulation that keeps the industry's finances perpetually under pressure.

Southwest, of course, has managed to avoid those cycles. For three decades, it's consistently achieved the stability for which other airlines continue to search.

Among many proposals for revamping the industry, Crandall called for new fare structures that encourage nonstop flights, something he calls the "sum of the locals." Basically, nonstops would cost less because they're less expensive to operate. Customers also prefer them.

Stopping Stops

If the strategy sounds familiar, it should. It's a lot like the point-to-point service Southwest has flown since 1973, a strategy that's one of the cornerstones of its sustained profitability.

Hubs, after all, exist not because they're better for passengers, but because they made the business easier for the airlines by funneling traffic to more profitable routes.

As rising fuel prices lead to growing desperation among the hub-and-spoke carriers, they may be more willing to abandon systems that still hearken back to the days of regulation.

As difficult as higher fuel prices are, they only exacerbate the industry's long-festering problems.

Southwest has actually increased its economic advantage over rivals this year because it hedged 70 percent of its fuel at $51 a barrel, Kelleher said.

As a result, it's been expanding as others, including Houston-based Continental [Airlines], are pruning routes, planes and employees.

Bitter Rivals

Southwest's growth apparently irritates some of its rivals. After an abysmal earnings announcement in April, United [Airlines] executives said that given higher fuel prices, the only "responsible" thing for carriers to do was to cut domestic capacity.

"You do have some significant low-cost carriers with growth in their plans, and it's hard to imagine how you make that work in this environment," United's chief revenue officer, John Tague, said at the time.

Southwest, of course, was adding flights at Denver and has been having no trouble making it work.

The fact that it makes it work better than anyone simply shows that deregulation wasn't an empty promise.

Southwest has its detractors, and its system has its flaws, but its rise up the list of largest airlines underscores deregulation's success.

The rest of the industry likes to dismiss Southwest as an anomaly, an unusual circumstance that doesn't reflect the industry norm.

The question, though, isn't why more carriers haven't thrived under deregulation, it's why so many inefficient ones have survived for so long.

> *"Far more damaging was the Airline Deregulation Act [of] 1978, which handed out financial bonanzas to shareholders—but, in the long term, led to less competition and thus poorer service."*

Deregulation Has Harmed the Airline Industry

Andrew Stephen

Andrew Stephen has written for a variety of newspapers, including the New York Times. *He is also U.S. editor of the* New Statesman.

In the following viewpoint, Stephen claims that deregulation has been harmful for both airlines and passengers. Deregulation has led to less competition and therefore poorer service within the airlines and caused many airlines to lose money and go into bankruptcy. Stephen relays incidences of passengers kept waiting on the tarmac for between five and ten hours and ultimately concludes that the U.S. airline industry is in a death spiral.

As you read, consider the following questions:

1. In 2007, how much money were U.S. airlines forecasted to lose?

2. According to Stephen, what percentage of U.S. Airways' revenue was spent on the workforce prior to the publication of his article? What percentage was spent in 2007, when the article was published?

3. What did Bruce Lakefield, then chief executive officer of U.S. Airways, say about deregulation in 2004?

British travellers beware: The US airline industry is in a tailspin, and passenger service and staff morale are hitting rock-bottom.

Yes, I've flown on Ryanair, easyJet, Flybe and so on, and I know they can be pretty ropy. I also know British Airways loses an awful lot of bags (more than any other major European airline, I'm told). Heathrow [Airport] can certainly be a disgrace.

But if anybody thinks flying to and from British airports is uniquely awful, I have news for them. In America, which boasts six of the world's biggest airlines, flying even on short-haul flights is beginning to get much, much worse—and the outlook is bleaker still. This year, airlines around the world are expected to make $3.8bn [billion] profit, with European firms accounting for $2.4bn of that and Asian-Pacific ones for most of the rest. The US airlines are forecast to *lose* $600m [million], and I expect the losses to end up being much more.

Figures just published by the Airline Quality Rating, the authoritative annual survey that examines the performance of 18 airlines using government statistics, found that last year more passengers were bumped from flights, more bags were lost and more flights arrived late than in the previous year. No less than a quarter of all US airline flights are late. Two of the Big Six—Delta and Northwest—are currently bankrupt (under

America's Chapter 11 regulations, which allow companies to declare bankruptcy but remain operating while, in theory, they get their act together)—and three of the remaining four have slipped in and out of bankruptcy in recent years.

"We're going to see more delays and those delays translate to cancellations, mishandled bags and unhappy passengers. It's not a pretty picture," says David Castelveter, spokesman for the Air Transport Association.

The Damage of Deregulation

Why? The 11 September 2001 atrocities [terrorist attacks] were certainly a big setback for all US airlines—but the [George W.] Bush administration handed out huge taxpayer bailouts to them, and problems arising from 9/11 largely dissipated after 2005. Far more damaging was the Airline Deregulation Act [of] 1978, which handed out financial bonanzas to shareholders—but, in the long term, led to less competition and thus poorer service. Two years later, Ronald Reagan famously dismissed 11,359 of the nation's 12,000 air-traffic controllers for going on strike; today the US air-traffic control system is antiquated and working far beyond its capacity.

The airlines I have to travel on most are US Airways and United—at the moment, I have 396,812 miles in my United Mileage account—and they are probably the worst of the six giants. US Airways is the smaller of the two, but still runs nearly 4,000 daily flights serving 240 destinations in 28 countries, with a workforce of more than 37,000; but it was bankrupt from 2002 to 2005, during which it not only tried to pare costs down to the bone, but sliced off slivers of the bone itself. Previously, roughly 40 per cent of its revenue was spent on the workforce, but that has now plunged to just 17 per cent— leading to a demoralised staff who care less and provide increasingly bad service.

Countless thousands of airline staff have found their treasured pensions disappear in smoke and their pay slashed in the "reorganisations"—and they are the lucky ones who have kept their jobs. "The entire industry is in a death spiral, including this company, and I can't get us out of it. Deregulation is an abysmal failure and we have no more furniture left to burn," Bruce Lakefield, then chief executive officer of US Airways, said in 2004. The following year, Lakefield took home what, to him, was doubtless the insultingly paltry sum of $2.2m.

United, which has 56,000 employees and operates a fleet of 459 aircraft, was bankrupt from 2002 until last year—and its service went from bad to dismal. Yet Glenn Tilton, the CEO who shepherded United into bankruptcy when the entire company was valued at just $20m, nevertheless managed to take home $39.7m last year. (Don't ask me to explain this sort of financial smoke-and-mirrors, because I can't: The wretched US Airways recently bid $9.77bn for Delta, a manoeuvre I find no less baffling.)

Nightmare stories for passengers and mere airline workers abound, while the fat cats enrich themselves. In February, passengers on ten planes belonging to JetBlue—a relatively small airline, but which nevertheless is now the biggest carrier operating out of New York's [John F.] Kennedy Airport, and which was found to be the country's second most efficient airline in the AQR survey—kept passengers on ten planes waiting on the tarmac for between five and a half and ten hours because of bad weather.

Last month, I found myself shepherding a party of six people, including four children, from Washington to Florida—going out on United and returning on US Airways. On the day we were to depart, moderate snowfall was forecast for New York. There was not a snowflake to be seen in Washington and nor was any snow forecast, but I received computerised e-mail and text messages seven hours before our scheduled departure saying something like (I can't remember the exact words): "Flight 1615 has been cancelled. You may have been rerouted, so it is vital that you immediately contact a United representative on 1-800-241-6522."

Infuriating Messages

I duly kept three phone lines open for four hours listening to infuriatingly cheerful recorded announcements, but could neither reach a human being nor get any automated information on the phone or online. The only alternative was to travel the 35 miles to Washington Dulles [International Airport]—which was a zoo, far worse than I have ever seen Heathrow. After queuing for nearly two hours, we were put on a flight two days hence—still with nary a snowflake to be seen outside. (We actually managed to get a flight the next day, but only after a little finessing from me.)

Coming back, US Airways failed to deliver my suitcase, something that has happened to me more in the past two years than in the previous three decades. I provided all relevant details and the all-important baggage tag and bar code to the airline's lost-luggage office and was told to go home—and then check online or phone a number. Back home I found online that US Airways was "still checking" for a bag that the airline apparently believed had no baggage tag number or bar code and belonged to a non-existent Ms Margaret A S Stephen. I then spent 90 minutes waiting on the phone to get through to a human being—and found he was in *Guatemala*, clueless, and doubtless being paid some truly pathetic pittance. My suitcase was clearly destined for the notorious 50,000-square-foot graveyard in Scottsboro, Alabama, where luggage lost and misidentified forever by US airlines is bought and sold off at the rate of more than 7,000 items a day.

Instinct and experience made me make three return trips to the airport that evening, where I asked a couldn't-care-less human being whether my bag had been scanned in at West Palm Beach. "Oh, we don't do that," she replied airily. On my third trip I clambered in among seas of suitcases and finally found mine, which had apparently come in on a later flight, and duly told the lost-luggage office. Four days later, Margaret Stephen was still being told online that US Airways was trying to find her suitcase—and *eight* days later I received a phone call (at least the company had my number right) asking whether Margaret had ever found her bag.

I had known this kind of rot was setting in two years ago, when I made a three-day trip to London on US Airways and my suitcase failed to materialise at Gatwick [Airport]. I spent £141 on basic toiletries and a change of clothes, knowing that under the 1929 Warsaw Convention and its updated 1999 Montreal replacement, I would be entitled to at least part of that as compensation for what turned out to be 48 hours without my belongings (British Airways paid Victoria Beckham £100,000 for one lost suitcase, after all). I had my suitcase for just one full day before I returned to the United States—where, surrealistically, US Airways managed to lose it yet again.

I thought that if I FedExed a letter direct to the aforementioned Lakefield with receipts for the £141, it would at least prompt a response. I am still waiting to hear a peep from Lakefield, now vice chairman, or anyone in his office, let alone receive a penny of the money the airline owes me—despite having a FedEx receipt showing that my letter was safely delivered and signed for.

Despite all that I have recounted above, the British government recently granted more US airlines the right to use Heathrow, a deal worth literally billions to the American airlines but little or nothing, as far as I can see, to Britain. American airlines have always been allowed to fly from New York to Frankfurt via London, say, and pick up invaluable new passengers in London. However, in what amounts to a scandalous breach of the free-enterprise ethos that Americans are supposed to hold so dear, the reverse does not apply: If British Airways flies from London to Dallas via Boston, say, the US denies it the right to pick up lucrative additional passengers in Boston, a blatant repudiation of the free-market system that costs the British airlines (again literally) billions.

The brand-new "open skies" agreement will allow American and European airlines to fly from any airport in Europe to any in America and vice versa, and that just may help the low-cost European airlines to compete against the American giants. I would perhaps give Ryanair a miss, but would much rather fly across the Atlantic with Flybe, say, than with any of the six US giants. Britain, as usual, is only slowly waking up to these realities of American life.

The truth is that you were dead right, Mr Lakefield: The US airline industry is in a death spiral. But I still have copies of my letter and those receipts, so perhaps it is not too late for you to recompense me with that £141—maybe even out of the paltry £2.2m to which you so selflessly limited yourself to that year.

> *"With one swift stroke, deregulation of international markets would spur competition on international routes and possibly eliminate a major motivation for some prospective mergers."*

The Airlines Should Be More Deregulated

Steven A. Morrison and Clifford Winston

Steven A. Morrison is professor and chair of the Department of Economics at Northeastern University. Clifford Winston is a senior fellow in the economic studies program of the Brookings Institution.

The deregulation of the airline industry has been a success, claim Morrison and Winston in the following viewpoint, pointing to lower fares, more flights, greater safety, and more efficient carriers to support their assertion. Although passengers have benefited from deregulation, airline profits have suffered. Further deregulation is needed in the airline industry to help carriers become more efficient and thus more profitable, the authors contend. Two ways of accomplishing this are through mergers and by deregulating international markets, they suggest.

Steven A. Morrison and Clifford Winston, "The State of Airline Competition and Prospective Mergers: Statements of Steven A. Morrison and Clifford Winston," Hearing before the Judiciary Committee Antitrust Task Force, United States House of Representatives, April 24, 2008. Reproduced by permission of the authors.

As you read, consider the following questions:

1. Why do the authors assert that competition may be at an all-time high?

2. According to Morrison and Winston's estimate, what percentage of airline seats were filled before deregulation?

3. What is the main motivation behind airline mergers, according to the authors?

This fall [2008] the United States will celebrate the 30th anniversary of the Airline Deregulation Act of 1978—and the nation does have reason to celebrate because airline deregulation has benefited both travelers and carriers. Among the most important benefits: fares have fallen significantly, flight frequency has increased, and carriers have become more efficient. Moreover, these benefits have been realized while air travel safety continues to improve.

However, it would be misleading to conclude that the industry's adjustment to deregulation—and the extent of deregulation—is complete. Airline industry earnings have fluctuated greatly since deregulation and the industry has yet to earn a normal rate of return on invested capital on a consistent basis. Accordingly, carriers continue to seek ways to reduce costs and increase profitability, especially in light of recent opportunities to expand their international operations as part of the March 2008 Open Skies agreement with the European Union [EU]. Further deregulation of international markets could occur through Open Skies agreements with countries outside of the EU.

Mergers are one strategy that some airlines have pursued to improve the efficiency of their networks and to expand their domestic and international route coverage. Recently, Northwest Airlines and Delta Air Lines have filed an application to merge their operations and it is expected that other merger proposals will follow. This testimony provides some perspective on the motivation for and likely effects of airline mergers in the context of the current state of airline competition. We also note some policies that would spur additional competition in the industry.

The State of Airline Competition

The standard way to measure airline competition is the number of effective competitors (i.e., equivalent equal-sized carriers) on a route. . . . [C]ompetition on all routes increased for several years after deregulation in 1978, and . . . it has fluctuated somewhat because of mergers in the late 1980s, the macroeconomic expansion in the late 1990s, and the 2001 terrorist attacks. Although . . . the number of competitors varies by route distance, in general, airline competition today is nearly as great as it ever was. In fact, competition may be at an all-time high because of the growth of low-cost carriers. That is, the intensity of competition on a route is determined by the number of airline carriers and the *identity* of the carriers. . . . [T]he percentage of passenger miles where low-cost carriers compete for traffic with legacy (i.e., pre-deregulation) carriers continues to increase.

The number and identity of airlines in city pair markets has been sufficient to cause real airline fares to continue their long-term decline. Of course, some travelers pay higher fares per mile than other travelers pay; but competitive pressures continue to keep real fares from rising. This fact is of particular importance for the current financial health of the industry because fuel prices have recently increased dramatically. As recently as 1998, jet fuel accounted for less than 10 percent of airline costs. So far this year [2008], it accounts for more than one-third of airline costs; thus, the industry is under additional pressure to reduce costs.

Competition unleashed by deregulation has caused airlines to become more efficient. In the decade before deregulation, load factors—or the percentage of seats filled with paying passengers—were around 55 percent. Load factors have increased since deregulation, indicating that airlines are making more efficient use of their available seat capacity. In the wake of September 11 [2001 terrorist attacks], carriers have not increased their seat capacity as fast as passenger demand has risen, resulting in load factors that have climbed to record levels of nearly 80 percent.

Given such high load factors, it would be expected that the U.S. airline industry would be making handsome profits, but that is not the case. In 2006 and 2007, the industry rebounded to a modest extent from its substantial losses following the September 11, 2001, terrorist attacks, only to report a loss in the first quarter of 2008.

Prospective Mergers

Given the current state of the macroeconomy and the recent increase in fuel prices, airlines are under increasing pressure to reduce costs and increase revenues. How do mergers fit into the picture?

In a 2000 paper, we analyzed the determinants of all the actual and attempted airline mergers since 1978. We found that carriers are generally not motivated to merge for anticompetitive reasons, but rather by the acquiring carriers' desire to expand their international routes—which are more profitable than most domestic routes due to government agreements that limit entry—and by the acquired carriers' need to be rescued from financial distress.

What about evidence on the effects of previous mergers on travelers? In the aforementioned paper, we found that the US Air-Piedmont merger and the Northwest-Republic and TWA-Ozark mergers, which were opposed by the Justice Department but approved by the U.S. Department of Transportation [DOT] (at the time DOT had jurisdiction in the matter), had benign effects on fares.

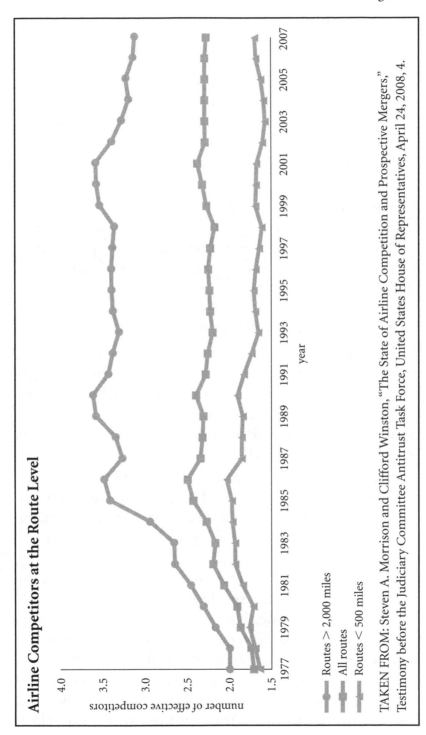

Airline Competitors at the Route Level

number of effective competitors

year

— Routes > 2,000 miles
— All routes
— Routes < 500 miles

TAKEN FROM: Steven A. Morrison and Clifford Winston, "The State of Airline Competition and Prospective Mergers," Testimony before the Judiciary Committee Antitrust Task Force, United States House of Representatives, April 24, 2008, 4.

In light of this evidence, the merger between Delta and Northwest appears to be motivated by the merged airline's desire to offer expanded international operations, to restructure its network to attract more business travelers in its traffic mix thus increasing revenues, and to achieve cost reductions by, for example, retiring older aircraft. It is highly unlikely that a merged Delta and Northwest would reduce competition on those routes that both carriers served (or could serve) because low-cost carriers tend to move very quickly to mitigate fare increases initiated by legacy carriers.

Generally, the effect on travelers of changes in airline market structure caused by mergers depends on the specific carriers that exit a market and the specific carriers that take their place.

Further Policy Considerations

Thus far we have confined our statement to mergers, which are intended to help airlines without harming travelers. Taking a broader perspective, policies exist that could have a beneficial impact on the welfare of air travelers by increasing competition on international and domestic routes, but industry earnings could be reduced.

With one swift stroke, deregulation of international markets would spur competition on international routes and possibly eliminate a major motivation for some prospective mergers. The recent Open Skies agreement with the EU is a positive step that should be replicated by the United States with all regions of the world. Government-mandated limits on foreign ownership of U.S. carriers should be eliminated, which would make it easier for struggling U.S. carriers to attract foreign capital to help solve their financial problems and possibly eliminate another major reason that carriers seek a merger.

Allowing foreign carriers to serve U.S. domestic routes (cabotage) would provide another source of competition that would benefit air travelers. Think of how foreign transplants have transformed the automobile and steel industries to the benefit of consumers. Still another source of competition could be developed by allowing foreign investors to establish a new U.S. carrier without any limits on foreign ownership of the carrier.

Finally, policy makers could potentially stimulate airline competition by experimenting with privatization of some U.S. airports, thereby allowing them to compete aggressively for air carrier service. Competitive entry at some airports is constrained by insufficient gates and terminal space. Given the contractual relationship governing publicly owned airports and the incumbent airlines that help pay their bonds, some airports have limited incentives to attract additional carriers.

| "Three decades of deregulation have demonstrated that airlines have special characteristics incompatible with a completely unregulated environment."

The Airlines Need More Regulation

Robert L. Crandall

Robert L. Crandall is the former chairman, president, and chief executive officer of AMR Corporation, the parent company of American Airlines.

There are certain industries in which deregulation simply doesn't work, states Crandall in the following viewpoint, and the airline industry is one of them. Allowing an unfettered free market system in the airline industry has created substandard airline service for passengers and an unprofitable marketplace for carriers. The rise in fuel prices alone is not the reason why airlines are struggling financially, Crandall claims, and allowing more mergers isn't the answer. The real problem is the way fares are priced, and there are nonintrusive ways for the government to help the industry regulate its pricing practices.

"Remarks of Robert L. Crandall," The Wings Club, June 10, 2008. Reproduced by permission of Robert L. Crandall.

As you read, consider the following questions:

1. What are some of the issues that Crandall cites to support his contention that airline service since deregulation has deteriorated?

2. What three reasons does Crandall cite for the problems facing airlines?

3. What approach does Crandall recommend to address both pricing and fuel issues?

Our airlines, once world leaders, are now laggards in every category, including fleet age, service quality and international reputation. Fewer and fewer flights are on time. Airport congestion has become a staple of late-night comedy shows. An ever-higher percentage of bags are lost or misplaced. Last-minute seats are harder and harder to find. Passenger complaints have skyrocketed. Airline service, by any standard, has become unacceptable.

Meanwhile, the financial health of the industry, and of the individual carriers, has become ever more precarious. Most have been through the bankruptcy process at least once, and some have passed through on multiple occasions.

An analyst from Mars just arrived and, knowing nothing of the industry's background, might be forgiven for believing that the entire problem can be laid at OPEC's doorstep. If only fuel prices were lower, the Martian might conclude, the industry would have no problem. Looking around the room, I see no Martians—but lots of folks who can remember—as I do—when the industry lost money while paying far less for fuel than it does today. While the price of fuel—and particularly the rapid rate at which it has risen—has certainly complicated the management challenge, it is clear that fuel prices are not the core of the problem.

Nor is inadequate scale. These days, the solution de jure seems to be mergers, and many voices clamor that consolidation is both inevitable and imperative. In my view, the arguments in favor of consolidation are unpersuasive. Mergers will not lower fuel prices. They will not increase economies of scale for already sizable major airlines. They will require major capital expenditures and are likely to increase labor costs. Finally, they will disadvantage many employees, whose incentive to provide good service will be further reduced.

If consolidation were really the answer, it is conceivable that the system could be run by a single efficient operator. However, consumers clearly benefit from the existence of multiple airlines; the absence of alternatives does not encourage good customer service. Thus, our goal should be to harness competition and regulation to create a system responsive to both the imperative of efficiency and the desirability of decent service.

As is always the case, "victory has many fathers, but failure is an orphan" and no one wants to take credit for the sad state of our aviation industry. Fortunately, there is plenty of blame to go around. In my view, the industry's problems reflect several shortcomings:

- First and foremost, we have failed to confront the reality that unfettered competition just doesn't work very well in certain industries, as amply demonstrated by our airline experience and by the adverse outcomes associated with various state efforts to deregulate electricity rates. In my view, it is time to acknowledge that airlines look and are more like utilities than ordinary businesses.

- Second, our government has failed to develop a national transportation plan of any kind and has thus been indifferent to the continuing decline of our highways, our railroads and our airlines.

- And third, the government has failed to invest in the capabilities and resources which only it can provide, most notably by failing to implement the new air traffic control system that everyone agrees we desperately need.

In my view, it's time to do something about all three.

I feel little need to argue that deregulation has worked poorly in the airline industry. Three decades of deregulation have demonstrated that airlines have special characteristics incompatible with a completely unregulated environment. To put things bluntly, experience has established that market forces alone cannot and will not produce a satisfactory airline industry, which clearly needs some help to solve its pricing, cost and operating problems.

It must now be clear to all that one of the industry's fundamental problems is the way in which it prices its product. As you all know, airlines work with a very distorted supply-demand equation. The instant perishability of empty seats, the impossibility of quickly reducing fixed and semi-variable costs when demand falters, the public's view that all airline seats are interchangeable commodities, the plethora of competitors and the desire to protect the reach of networks all create a great temptation to sustain volume by selling seats too cheaply.

In addition to producing huge losses, current pricing and operating practices have produced many negative side effects. In an effort to ameliorate losses, airlines have driven load factors much higher than can comfortably be managed; have outsourced much of their labor to firms employing marginally capable personnel; have introduced hundreds of small, inefficient aircraft; have eliminated amenities once considered normal; and are imposing a wide range of fees to supplement revenue. The proliferation of fees irritates already unhappy customers, and some—notably baggage-checking fees—slow up the check-in process and encourage passengers to carry aboard even more than they have in the past.

I have heard various proposals for solving the pricing problem. The most aggressive favor government supervised

The Annual Earnings of US Airlines, 1955–2007

Year	Net Profit ($ million)	Net Profit Margin (%)	Cumulative Profit ($ 000)
1955	76	5.6	381,786
1956	80	4.6	461,448
1957	44	1.9	505,878
1958	50	3.0	556,274
1959	73	3.4	628,955
1960	9	0.0	638,095
1961	(38)	−1.7	600,221
1962	52	0.4	652,540
1963	78	0.5	731,020
1964	223	4.8	954,192
1965	367	6.8	1,321,311
1966	428	6.5	1,748,944
1967	415	5.5	2,164,332
1968	210	2.5	2,374,284
1969	53	1.8	2,427,036
1970	(201)	−1.6	2,226,533
1971	28	0.0	2,254,540
1972	215	2.5	2,469,391
1973	227	1.8	2,696,084
1974	322	2.1	3,017,725
1975	(84)	−1.8	2,933,521
1976	563	2.0	3,496,875
1977	753	2.7	4,249,411
1978	1,197	3.6	5,445,948
1979	347	1.3	5,792,793
1980	17	0.1	5,810,207
1981	(301)	−0.8	5,509,381
1982	(916)	−2.5	4,593,567
1983	(188)	−0.5	4,405,516
1984	825	1.9	5,230,184
1985	863	1.8	6,092,899
1986	(235)	−0.5	5,857,990
1987	593	1.0	6,451,388

continued

The Annual Earnings of US Airlines, 1955–2007
[CONTINUED]

Year	Net Profit ($ million)	Net Profit Margin (%)	Cumulative Profit ($ 000)
1988	1,686	2.6	8,136,987
1989	128	0.2	8,264,889
1990	(3,921)	−5.1	4,343,887
1991	(1,940)	−2.6	2,403,730
1992	(4,791)	−6.1	(2,387,554)
1993	(2,136)	−2.5	(4,523,180)
1994	(344)	0.4	(4,867,295)
1995	2,314	2.4	(2,553,704)
1996	2,727	2.8	173,360
1997	5,119	4.7	5,291,890
1998	4,847	4.3	10,139,368
1999	5,277	4.5	15,416,458
2000	2,486	1.9	17,902,756
2001	(8,275)	−7.2	9,627,890
2002	(11,008)	−10.6	(1,380,525)
2003	(2,371)	−3.1	(3,751,634)
2004	(7,643)	−6.9	(11,394,808)
2005	(5,782)	−3.8	(17,176,818)
2006	3,123	1.9	(14,053,546)
2007	4,998	2.9	(9,055,654)

TAKEN FROM: Air Transport Association, Geoffrey Thomas, "Deregulation's Mixed Legacy," *Air Transport World*, August 2008.

pricing discussions whose goal would be to establish minimum fares sufficient to cover full costs and produce a reasonable return. While I would fully support such an approach, the idea is deeply offensive to those who cling to the belief that the markets can solve everything.

However, I think there may be a less intrusive way for government to help the industry achieve compensatory pricing while simultaneously responding to the increasingly pressing need to increase its fuel efficiency. Suppose for a moment that in a world where every airline set its own prices, a regulatory agency required that any passenger traveling between two points via a connecting point pay the sum of the local fares on his or her itinerary.

As we have all known for many years, the cheapest way to carry a passenger from point A to point B is nonstop, and the most efficient way to do it is by using the largest airplane compatible with demand. To my mind, a "sum of the locals" rule would likely reduce the ability and motivation of airlines to preserve connecting complexes now being sustained by operating small, relatively inefficient aircraft, or by pricing connecting itineraries far below actual costs or—in far too many cases—doing both!!!! Ask yourself this: If the nonstop fare from Detroit to Los Angeles is $450, why should a passenger be able to travel via a connection for the same amount or, as is the case today, for even less?

In a sum of the locals world—or even in a world where the minimum fare was the nonstop price plus a connection premium—there might be fewer flights from Detroit to various hubs because higher through and connecting fares would mute demand. Passengers traveling only from Detroit to one of the hubs would likely have fewer service choices while passengers traveling to Los Angeles or other points beyond the hubs would confront a new paradigm in which the lower price of a nonstop journey might make waiting for a nonstop more desirable than choosing a higher cost but more convenient departure via a connecting point.

This argument, of course, turns the conventional wisdom about hubs on its head. However, times are very different now than they were when the hub-and-spoke system was growing rapidly. In those days, the United States gave little thought to either global warming or energy independence; today, the U.S. spends $600 billion per year on petroleum, pines for energy independence and watches the ice caps with increasing trepidation.

Things have changed dramatically and will change even more in the years ahead. In due course, our country's need for energy conservation and our airline's need for profitability will inevitably generate an intensive search for new approaches. . . .

The carriers also need help in curbing labor costs. As everyone here knows, airline efforts to control labor costs have been blunted—since the demise of the mutual aid pact in 1978—by the dramatic imbalance between the negotiating strength of organized labor and that of the airlines. Unlike industries with a tangible product, airline seats cannot be stockpiled. Thus, an airline has no product to sell during a strike, loses business when a strike is threatened, and suffers from reduced traffic for months after a strike is settled. Moreover, airlines are unable to quickly reduce fixed and semi-fixed costs during a strike. Thus, as a practical matter, no airline can endure a strike and will invariably yield to labor's demands before a strike is actually called.

The result has been labor rates and work rules which are far more generous than those offered for comparable skills in other industries. Since strikes against transportation utilities are illegal in many jurisdictions around the world and are clearly contrary to the public interest, I do not see why the Railway Labor Act should not be amended to require binding arbitration. While organized labor would object to being deprived of its ultimate weapon, it seems likely that the threat of binding arbitration would encourage both labor and management to adopt more moderate positions than has been true in the past while simultaneously moving all airlines closer to labor cost parity.

We would also be well advised to revise our bankruptcy laws to deprive failed carriers of the right to use lower costs to undercut the fares offered by their more prudent rivals. Forcing both management and labor to face the twin specters of liquidation and unemployment would likely be another step towards less confrontation and more cooperation.

It is also clear that decisive government action is needed to relieve the extreme congestion now being experienced at our busiest airports. As we all know, airlines cannot unilaterally reduce frequencies because doing so would allow another carrier the opportunity to add flights and gain a competitive advantage. In the short term, the only solution is a regulatory mandate that limits the number of flights scheduled to what the runways, terminals, and air traffic control facilities at a given airport can handle. . . .

The government should also tighten the financial standards that must be met by new airlines. In the years since deregulation, nearly 200 airlines have come and gone. These inadequately financed carriers, whose principal goal has often seemed limited to either lasting long enough to reap the rewards of an initial public offering or satisfying the ego of yet another would-be airline mogul, have consistently cut prices to attract passengers. Such short-term antics have destabilized the pricing structure required by a healthy industry, and have offered no lasting benefit to anyone.

Finally, we should ask ourselves whether using our antitrust laws to prevent airlines from collaborating to achieve more intensive asset utilization and more efficient operations really makes sense. It is hard to imagine the kind of clean slate productivity gains that are clearly needed without some relaxation of past and present restraints on cooperation.

Modest price regulation, slot controls at congested airports, more stringent standards for new carriers, revised labor laws, amended bankruptcy statutes, and a more accommodating stance towards industry collaboration are a far cry from the inclusive regulatory regime of the CAB days. However, these few steps—in my view—would have a dramatic and favorable impact on the financial health of our airlines, the usefulness of our airline system, service levels in the airline business, and the welfare of airline employees.

| *"True deregulation involves allowing market actors to run their businesses in whatever manner they like, price what the market will bear, and discover for themselves how best to deliver goods and services."*

True Deregulation of Electric Power Would Benefit Consumers

Jerry Taylor and Peter Van Doren

Jerry Taylor is a senior fellow and director of natural resource studies at the Cato Institute. Peter Van Doren is editor of Regulation, *a magazine published by the Cato Institute.*

Unlike other industries in which deregulation has resulted in lower prices for consumers, electric power rates have increased, causing many to point to deregulation as the culprit, claim Taylor and Van Doren in the following viewpoint. However, what we have in the power market is not true deregulation, argue the authors, stating that any benefits arising from price deregulation have been offset by regulations in other areas. True deregulation allows companies to run their businesses as they see fit, pricing and providing their services without government interference. We don't have that environment in the electric power market, the authors contend, and that is the real cause of the problem.

As you read, consider the following questions:

1. What industries do the authors cite as examples of deregulation lowering prices for consumers?

2. What was the real impetus for deregulation in the electric power market, according to the authors?

3. The authors claim that under deregulation, higher prices during peak times would be offset by lower prices during off-peak times. What evidence do they cite to back this claim?

After a pretty good 30-year run, deregulation is on the political ropes. Although loosening the shackles on banking, trucking and airlines delivered lower prices, robust competition and political applause, it hasn't worked for electricity. California and Virginia have already abandoned the project and other states are contemplating a similar retreat. For the first time in decades, Americans are inclined to think that regulation is the thin blue line between defenseless consumers and predatory capitalists.

Why Rates Increased

So did free market reformers take deregulation too far? Yes and no.

Yes, because they promised rate reductions they had no business promising. No, because deregulation of some parts of the system was offset by more ambitious regulations elsewhere. The end result is even more economically artificial than the one we started with.

Many of the states that undertook utility restructuring in the late 1990s rolled back retail electricity prices and then froze them in place for years during the "transition" to retail competition. The headline-grabbing rate increases this year [2007] in Maryland (50% in Baltimore) and Illinois (24% in Chicago) occurred because the period of regulated prices ended—while during the freeze period the prices of the fuels used for generation (coal and natural gas) increased significantly.

The states sticking to the old regulatory regime had no rate freezes, instead passing on higher fuel costs to consumers through gradual price increases. The average increase in rates in the regulated states from 1990 through 2006 (one cent per kWh [kilowatt-hour]) is not statistically different from the increase in deregulated states (1.6 cents per kWh).

Still, electricity rates increased under deregulation, while rates decreased in deregulated industries like airlines, banking and trucking. Why?

Under the old regulatory regime, electricity generators received their costs plus an allowed return on capital. If generators' costs differed, they received differing revenues. Prices were then established by a "weighted average" of all producer costs. Under deregulation, however, generators receive revenues based on the price charged by the most expensive generator whose output is necessary to meet demand in each hour.

While some may find such pricing to be odd, it is found in all commodity markets. Potatoes, for example, sell at the same price even though the cost of production varies across farmers. The supermarket does not price potatoes based on the "weighted average" of their acquisition costs, and producers do not sell at cost plus a modest markup. They sell at what the market will bear, and the market will bear the highest cost source of potatoes necessary to meet consumer demand.

Thus, in a regulatory regime, rising natural gas prices affect electricity prices only according to the percentage of electricity generated by natural gas (about 18.7% of supply nationwide in 2005). But in deregulated markets, all generators get revenues based on the price charged by the most expensive (often natural gas) plant in operation.

Does this mean that consumers are always worse off under market (marginal-cost) prices rather than regulated (weighted-average) prices? Well, regulation certainly delivers lower prices than the market during shortages. But regulation delivers higher prices during times of relative abundance.

Deregulation Was Meant to Protect Producers

Few remember that the impetus for deregulation was the discrepancy between higher-priced "regulated" power (predominantly coal and nuclear) and lower-priced spot market power (predominantly from gas-fired power plants) when natural gas costs were low in the 1990s. The owners of coal and nuclear generation resisted market pricing because they believed (correctly at that time) that in a market-price regime they would not recover the capital costs of their much more capital-intensive generation.

Thus rate freezes in states "deregulating" electricity markets were not designed to protect consumers. They were meant to protect high-cost producers, and kept retail prices from falling, if the new markets were driven by marginal-cost pricing.

Still, markets appear to be worse than regulation because generators whose costs are lower than the most expensive players in the market will get "excess" revenues. But excess profits aren't forever. Once returns are predictably higher than normal, entry will occur to dissipate them.

Consider Texas. Unlike other deregulated states, utilities in Texas were allowed to pass fuel-cost increases on to consumers on a yearly basis during the transition to full deregulation. There was no provision, however, for passing through fuel-cost *decreases*. Post-Katrina [a hurricane in 2005], natural gas prices pushed the cost of electricity to between 15 cents and 19 cents per kWh. But electricity prices did not adjust down when natural gas prices fell.

Those high prices, which result in large profits for coal-fired plants, induced TXU [Energy], the largest generator in Texas, to announce plans to build 11 more coal plants. Ironically, the much-praised plan by Kohlberg Kravis Roberts & Co. to take over TXU and build only three coal-fired power plants will keep power costs higher than otherwise. Environmentalists and plant owners win while ratepayers lose.

Deregulation Benefits Consumers

A final worry is that deregulation means sky-high prices during peak demand periods, typically hot summer afternoons. True. But they would be more than offset by lower off-peak prices. That's because in a regulatory regime ratepayers must still pay off, through higher rates, the capital costs of power plants sitting idle during off-peak demand periods. And there's a lot of idle generating capacity. MIT [Massachusetts Institute of Technology] economist Paul Joskow, for example, reports that in New England during 2001, 45% of the generating capacity produced only 7% of the total electricity.

In sum, allowing markets to dictate electricity prices is a good thing for consumers, even if they are sometimes higher than under regulation. Unfortunately—and here is the fly in the ointment—price deregulation has been accompanied by rules encouraging the legal separation of generation from transmission and the purchase of wholesale power through organized spot markets.

This approach is based on the belief that, while the generating sector is potentially quite competitive, the electricity transmission business is not. Thus, the argument goes, deregulation, in order to work properly, must sever the vertical integration of electricity generation, transmission, and distribution under a single corporate umbrella.

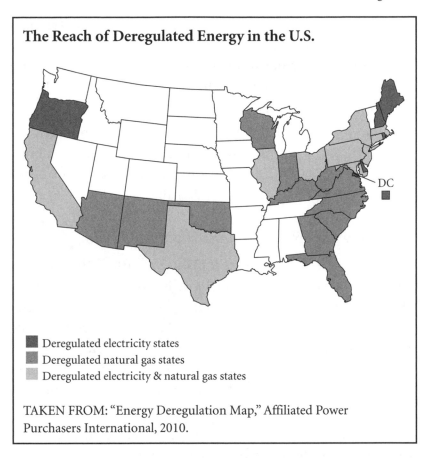

The Reach of Deregulated Energy in the U.S.

DC

■ Deregulated electricity states
■ Deregulated natural gas states
□ Deregulated electricity & natural gas states

TAKEN FROM: "Energy Deregulation Map," Affiliated Power
Purchasers International, 2010.

While this seems reasonable, there are good reasons why
vertical integration makes sense in the electric power business.
Unfortunately, none of those reasons have been given much of
a hearing.

First, vertical integration is an efficient response to the so-
called "holdup" problem. Investors in generating plants worry
that, because the assets are costly, dedicated and immobile,
they can be "held up" by transmission line owners. Investors
in transmission lines fear being held up by generators. Vertical
integration ends the fight.

Second, transmission and generation are substitutes for
one another—and the right amount of investment in either is
an economic, not an engineering, puzzle. Efficient investment

in both may not be possible through decentralized arrangements (prices and contracts) between separately owned assets. In contrast, an organization that owns both generation and transmission assets is more likely to invest optimally in both.

Third and finally, vertical integration minimizes risk in the real-time operation of the system. The better coordinated are generation and transmission, the less chance there is of cascading blackouts and other problems. Coordination is far easier when there is one actor rather than hundreds.

Balancing Firms' and Consumers' Interests

These considerations largely explain why 10 of the 11 published studies on this issue conclude that vertical integration is the most efficient corporate organizational form for electricity providers. Unfortunately, the debate about utility restructuring has almost completely ignored those studies—assuming rather that vertical integration serves no useful purpose other than facilitating the market power of incumbent electricity providers.

Interestingly enough, the deregulators are trying to create a world that would probably never arise in a totally free electricity market. In a world of deregulated vertically integrated firms, both producers and consumers would almost certainly resist spot market relationships. During gluts, firms would not recover the cost of capital; and during shortages, electricity consumers would be vulnerable to economic extortion, as competitive entry and rivalry can't happen overnight. Both firms and consumers would likely prefer long-term contracts, an arrangement that meets consumers' interest in price protection and firms' interest in cost recovery.

Accordingly, the equilibrium relationship between firms and consumers in a totally unregulated world might resemble that of the old regulatory regime, albeit an equilibrium achieved through contract. The only (unanswerable) question is how different the specifics of such hypothetical contracts would be from current regulatory practices.

True deregulation involves allowing market actors to run their businesses in whatever manner they like, price what the market will bear, and discover for themselves how best to deliver goods and services without government influencing those decisions with carrots and sticks. The faux deregulation we have in the electricity market unfortunately falls short on most of those counts. And that—rather than the rate increases—is the real problem.

> *"It turns out that in a deregulated market, the incentive is for generators to build too few plants rather than too many, creating periods of tight supply and very high prices."*

The Deregulation of Electric Power Does Not Benefit Consumers

Steven Pearlstein

Steven Pearlstein is a columnist for the Washington Post *who won the Pulitzer Prize for Commentary in 2008.*

While electric power deregulation may have helped the utilities, it has not benefited consumers, maintains Pearlstein in the following viewpoint, citing price increases of approximately 70 percent in the Maryland market. Part of the problem, he suggests, is that there are few markets with genuine competition. Consumers haven't shown an interest in shopping around for the best prices, and rate caps during the transition period discouraged new companies from entering a market. Although there are few clear answers about the fate of deregulation in the electric

Steven Pearlstein, "Deregulation's Unkept Promise," *The Washington Post*, June 1, 2007, p. D-1. Copyright © 2007 The Washington Post. Reprinted with permission.

power markets, many believe that the answer lies in a hybrid model combining some regulations in a competitive market environment.

As you read, consider the following questions:

1. What is the big driver behind Maryland's rate increases, in the author's view?

2. Who does Pearlstein say has benefited from deregulation?

3. What would be some of the features in the hybrid model Pearlstein describes?

Good morning, Maryland. It's June 1 [2007], and your electric bill is about go up again. Depending on where you live, the increases have been spread over two years or four, but the impact is the same: roughly, a 70 percent jump in the typical residential bill since price caps were lifted. So we'll understand if you're feeling a bit grumpy right now about electric power deregulation.

Deregulation Has Resulted in Higher Prices

The idea was that if competition were injected in the system—if power generation were separated from power distribution and customers could shop around for the best deal—prices would fall. In fact, people were so convinced the market would do a better job than regulators and monopoly suppliers that rates in Maryland were immediately cut 7 percent and capped at that level several years after that.

But now that things haven't worked out as planned, Maryland is rethinking the whole deregulation experiment. And no doubt Marylanders are looking longingly across the Potomac [River] to Virginia, which never fully embraced competition and has now decided to return to the good old days of the regulated monopoly. Beginning next month [July 2007], customers of Dominion [an energy producer] in northern Virginia will be paying about 9.75 cents per kilowatt-hour for their juice, 40 percent less than their neighbors in Maryland. (Pepco's customers in the District [of Columbia] are in between, paying about 11.5 cents per kilowatt-hour.)

To be fair, the big driver of Maryland's rate increases is simply the sharp rise in the cost of generating fuels, particularly oil and natural gas, since deregulation began. And Virginia's advantage comes in no small part because Dominion relies on cheaper coal and nuclear plants for more than two-thirds of its power.

But there is also no denying that deregulation has failed to live up to its promise, in Maryland and elsewhere.

Not that there haven't been some winners. The big push for deregulation came from big industrial customers who figured they could negotiate better deals on the wholesale market—and have. Also driving the deregulation bandwagon were the utilities themselves, which figured they could earn bigger profits if allowed to sell their power into an unregulated wholesale market, or sell their plants to some other company that would. While some have stumbled, most have been able to turn deregulation into a plus for their shareholders.

Why Deregulation Hasn't Helped Customers

There are various reasons why deregulation has failed to yield much benefit for customers.

Consumers, it turns out, just aren't very interested in shopping around for electric power. The difference in price just isn't worth the hassle. And because of the rate caps that many states, including Maryland, imposed during the transition period, it was difficult for new companies to enter the market with rates lower than those offered by the traditional utilities.

The result is that there are only a few markets with the innovative and robust competition envisioned by the early

champions of deregulation. And many now acknowledge that the retail side of the business is likely to remain a regulated monopoly.

The other key feature of the market-based model was requiring utilities to spin off or sell their generating plants. For years, critics had argued that, because they were guaranteed a rate of return, utilities had a financial incentive to build too many gold-plated power plants and run them inefficiently. But it turned out that they were only half right.

Under deregulation, individual plants are indeed operating at lower cost and greater efficiency. That's the good news. But it turns out that in a deregulated market, the incentive is for generators to build too few plants rather than too many, creating periods of tight supply and very high prices that can have a very distorted effect on wholesale markets.

Back in 2001, this was a particular problem in California, where the architects of deregulation had foolishly required all utilities to buy all their power on the day-ahead spot market. All it took was a summer heat wave to drive prices to record levels and cause an economic and political meltdown. Only later did we discover that the tight market was made even tighter by energy traders at Enron [an energy company] and other firms colluding to keep prices high by withholding supply from the market.

To avoid repeating California's mistakes, many states required utilities to buy power through long-term contracts at tightly structured and closely monitored auctions. Unfortunately for Maryland, one of its first such auctions came just as the impact of Hurricane Katrina was hitting energy markets [in 2005], locking in high prices for several years. And while Maryland regulators continue to tinker with the rules governing how and when utilities buy power, it remains unclear whether utilities save more money buying power through long-term contracts than by generating at least some power at their own plants.

A Way Forward

If there is any consensus these days, it is that the industry is evolving toward a hybrid model, somewhere between regulation and market competition. And within that context, much of the focus is on finding the most effective mechanisms for getting both residential and commercial customers to reduce their demand for power during peak hours, when the cost of producing or purchasing power is highest. Recent experiments show that even small reductions in peak load demand can yield large reductions in average rates.

Both Maryland and Virginia are now considering various mechanisms for reducing peak demand. Regulation-minded advocates like the idea of giving rebates to customers for buying energy-saving appliances and thermostats.

Market-oriented types, on the other hand, prefer some system of variable pricing, where the cost of electricity goes up during peak hours and peak days. Such a pricing scheme would require a huge investment in expensive new meters that can record how much power is consumed, hour by hour. Whether that investment will be worth it, however, depends on whether customers will have enough interest or incentive to turn off lights and adjust thermostats when prices are high. And like much about deregulation, that remains an open question.

> "Consumers have benefited from the de-
> regulation that has occurred, however
> haltingly at times, in the communica-
> tions marketplace since passage of the
> Telecommunications Act of 1996."

Telecommunications Deregulation Has Benefited Consumers

Randolph J. May

Randolph J. May is president of the Free State Foundation, an independent free market–oriented policy institute in Potomac, Maryland.

Telecommunications deregulation has benefited consumers, contends May in the following viewpoint, and any attempts to reverse deregulation in this industry should be resisted. Greater competition in telecommunications has resulted in innovative services, technological advancements, and competitive prices. However, May suggests that the Federal Communications Commission (FCC) has not always lived up to its self-described role as market facilitator rather than industry regulator. It should follow down the path toward helping to create and sustain market competition, he concludes, rather than resorting to regulation.

As you read, consider the following questions:

1. What data does May cite to support his assertion that deregulation has benefited consumers?

2. How does the FCC's clinging to its role as regulator harm consumers, according to the author?

3. What example does the author cite where the FCC could assist in fostering competition?

The financial services bailout threatens to give all deregulatory efforts a bad name. And it threatens to give those who reflexively favor more regulation, regardless of the marketplace circumstances, a new regulatory cudgel. If this reflexive approach is applied to today's communications marketplace, this would be most unfortunate. Consumers have benefited from the deregulation that has occurred, however haltingly at times, in the communications marketplace since passage of the Telecommunications Act of 1996. There is now competition among providers of broadband service in most parts of the country, and these providers offer an array of innovative Internet, video, and voice services over constantly evolving wireline, cable, wireless and satellite technologies.

The FCC's Strategic Plan

Even confronted with the reality of competitive communications markets, there remain many who want to reverse the regulatory relaxation that already has occurred, or even to impose entirely new regulations. In considering such calls, a brief look back is instructive. In August 1999, under the leadership of then Chairman William [E.] Kennard, the Federal Communications Commission [FCC] released a "Strategic Plan: A New FCC for the 21st Century."

In its first sentence, the strategic plan forecasts: "In five years, we expect U.S. communications markets to be characterized predominately by vigorous competition that will greatly reduce the need for direct regulation."

So the FCC proposed transitioning itself "from an industry regulator to a market facilitator." The notion that a market characterized predominately by vigorous competition needs market facilitation is questionable. But at least the plan's focus on creating and sustaining additional competition, rather than resorting to traditional regulation, was sensible.

Now [in late 2008], almost a decade later, it is useful to recall the agency's 1999 strategic vision, if only for the purpose of assessing knee-jerk calls for more regulation. The commission's prediction turned out to be correct. Communications markets, including broadband, are now generally competitive, driven largely by the ongoing technological advancements that characterize the digital revolution. Changing the agency's regulatory mind-set, in the face of institutional bureaucratic imperatives, has proven more difficult.

The FCC Has Not Lived Up to Its Mission

The FCC has reported that, as of June 2007, the most recent period for which its data are available, 96 percent of the nation's zip codes had two or more broadband providers. The rapid expansion in the availability of broadband service has not come cheap. Cable operators have spent well more than $100 billion upgrading their systems to handle digital broadband since passage of the 1996 telecom act. Determined to remain competitive, AT&T and Verizon reportedly have spent more than $70 billion in the last two years to expand capacity with fiber optic technology and other capacity-enhancing equipment.

As a result, in many communities across the nation cable operators and telephone companies are locked in fierce battles to attract and retain broadband Internet subscribers. These competitive battles often involve price reductions for stand-alone broadband service and discounts for the popular "triple play" bundled package of Internet, voice and video.

In truth, the FCC thus far has failed to do enough to change its role from "industry regulator" to "market facilitator." This failure harms consumers because continuation of legacy command-and-control regulation stifles investment and innovation.

The FCC's recent forays into net neutrality regulation are examples of inappropriate clinging to a legacy regulatory role. By its terms, net neutrality regulation, like traditional public utility regulation in monopolistic markets, requires the service provider to operate in a strictly nondiscriminatory manner. In 2007, when the FCC auctioned prime wireless frequencies, it required the auction winner to operate under net neutrality regulation, even though the wireless market is competitive.

The commission ignored the point that, in a competitive market, service providers will be driven to satisfy consumer demand in the most economically efficient manner. Otherwise, they will be punished by consumers.

Rather than allowing the market to perform its function, in that instance the agency adopted an "industry regulator" role. And, acting as industry regulator, the FCC recently sanctioned Comcast for conduct the company had reason to believe constituted reasonable network management practices.

The FCC Should Facilitate Competition

The FCC should be facilitating creation of even more facilities-based competition. A case in point is the pending proposal by Sprint Nextel and Clearwire to build a new broadband network using WiMAX, a new wireless technology. Even though the proposed service may not be substitutable in all respects for services provided by existing broadband providers, the added competition from the new WiMAX network should lead to lower prices and improved broadband service.

In 2000, not long after the release of the FCC's strategic plan, then FCC Commissioner Michael Powell declared: "Our bureaucratic process is too slow to respond to the challenges of Internet time." Internet time has become faster since, but FCC bureaucratic processes haven't. If the agency is to be a "market facilitator," it will need to render decisions in a more timely manner. Acting on the Sprint-Clearwire applications without delay is a good place to start.

Admittedly the FCC is not always confronted with an either-or choice—industry regulator versus market facilitator. There are instances in which regulation is warranted. But the key point is this: By focusing much more on a market facilitation role, the commission can foster additional marketplace competition that lessens the need for continuing a direct regulatory role. Once the Sprint-Clearwire applications for a new network are granted, for instance, calls for continuing to impose legacy regulation in the form of net neutrality mandates will be weaker still.

When the FCC is further along in the transition from industry regulator to market facilitator, it will be closer to embodying the "model agency for the digital age" envisioned by the 1999 strategic plan. The commission should not be deterred by those who seek to tar all deregulatory efforts by whatever regulatory intervention may be justified in the financial markets.

> *"California consumers have experienced an ongoing stream of rate increases, with the most recent increases for basic service. . . . 'Pricing freedom' for telephone companies has turned into a travesty for consumers."*

Telecommunications Deregulation Has Not Benefited Consumers

Trevor R. Roycroft

Trevor R. Roycroft was associate professor in the J. Warren Mc-Clure School of Information and Telecommunication Systems at Ohio University from 1994 to 2004. He represents clients before state and federal agencies, publishes research on telecommunications and information technology, and provides expert testimony in litigation involving telecommunications.

Telecommunications deregulation has been a disaster for consumers in California, argues Roycroft in the following viewpoint, based on a study conducted by The Utility Reform Network (TURN). Market competition was supposed to result in lower prices and better service for consumers. Instead, according to Roycroft, greater consolidation in the telecommunications industry has given consumers fewer choices of providers. As a result, telecommunications companies have raised prices. Among other remedies, the author calls for increased regulation.

As you read, consider the following questions:

1. According to the author, why did the California Public Utilities Commission remove pricing caps from the telecommunications market in California?

2. What is one of the mistaken assumptions on which the California Public Utilities Commission based its decision to lift pricing caps?

3. Outline one of the author's suggestions for the CPUC to reverse deregulation.

In August of 2006 the California Public Utilities Commission (CPUC) found that the states' four largest telephone companies "no longer possess market power" based on "the demonstrated presence of competitors" throughout their service territories. As a result, the CPUC has proceeded to dismantle almost all aspects of telecommunications regulation in California. Most significantly, the CPUC granted the state's dominant incumbent local exchange carriers (AT&T, Verizon, SureWest, and Citizens/Frontier) "broad pricing freedoms concerning almost all telecommunications services, new telecommunications products, bundles of services, promotion, and contracts."

However, instead of price competition, California consumers have experienced an ongoing stream of rate increases, with the most recent increases for basic service likely to cost consumers over $100 million per year. "Pricing freedom" for telephone companies has turned into a travesty for consumers, and the "competition" identified by the CPUC has turned out to be a myth.

In order to investigate the outcomes of the CPUC's deregulatory policy, TURN [The Utility Reform Network] commissioned a study of market conditions in California. This study, [Why "Competition" Is Failing to Protect Consumers:] The Limits of Choice in California's Residential Telecommunications Market, clearly demonstrates that contrary to CPUC assumptions, consumers have extremely limited choices of telephone service providers and that the "pricing freedom" granted to the incumbent telephone carriers has resulted in an ongoing stream of rate hikes driving prices sky-high.

Rate Increases Demonstrate Market Power

The CPUC's decision to remove the price cap framework that had previously protected consumers from market power was driven by the conclusion that "competition" would protect consumers. In other words, the market would self-regulate, and no firm would impose arbitrary rate increases on consumers. The CPUC accepted the conclusions of telephone company experts, such as Dr. Robert Harris, an economist who testified on behalf of AT&T California (formerly known as SBC).

Dr. Harris told the CPUC:

> One of the reasons I'm confident in making the recommendations that I'm making to this Commission (i.e., to remove price caps) is that I'm firmly convinced that the stupidest thing SBC or Verizon could do was think, oh, we got some pricing flexibility now. Let's start jacking up local service rates.

However, this is precisely what has occurred. Most recently, AT&T California and Verizon, the state's two largest telephone service providers, implemented, respectively, 23% and 13% increases for basic service rates. These rate increases alone are likely to cost California consumers more than $100 million per year. These most recent rate increases come on top of other increases by AT&T California and other large telephone companies. Price increases of the magnitude implemented by AT&T California and other telephone companies are not consistent with a "self-regulating" market where competition protects consumers.

This ongoing stream of price increases should be a wake-up call to the CPUC that self-regulation has failed to deliver the consumer protection that price caps had previously provided.

Price Increases and the Limits of Choice

The TURN study finds that market competition is failing to protect consumers. Not surprisingly, given the rate increases that have been imposed by telephone companies, the study finds that wireline telephone service has unique characteristics that are difficult to substitute for alternative voice technologies such as wireless services or voice over Internet protocol (VoIP) services. Because there are limits on consumers' ability to choose, telephone companies have found it profitable to "jack up rates."

The study finds that numerous factors contribute to the ability of telephone companies to increase rates. For example, the CPUC, in deciding to lift price caps, relied heavily on the conclusion that wireless mobility services are a close substitute for wireline telephone service. The study finds substantial evidence that this is not the case. . . .

Choices Are Increasingly Limited

The CPUC, when deciding to lift price caps, identified competitive local exchange carriers (CLECs) as an important source of competition. The report finds that CLEC competition has declined dramatically since the CPUC issued its decision—there are now over 50% fewer CLEC lines in service compared to the peak of CLEC operations. The two largest residential CLECs, MCI and the legacy AT&T, merged with

Verizon and SBC (now known as the new AT&T). Given this decline in competition, it is not surprising to find residential rates rising.

The report also finds that while some cable television companies have begun to offer voice telephone services, there are substantial limitations on the ability of these services to constrain telephone company price increases. . . .

These [limitations] reduce consumers' ability to choose alternatives to their local telephone company's service. If consumers have limits on their ability to choose alternatives, price increases are more likely.

The report conducted research to identify the choices that California consumers can make among alternative providers of wireline telephone services, and found that most Californians are likely to have two choices—service available from their local telephone company (either service packages or à la carte options), or service available from their local cable company (typically a service package). The report studied these alternatives in nine California counties, where nearly 50% of California's population resides. . . .

In and around urban areas, cable voice services are available, giving consumers one alternative to the local telephone company, while those consumers residing outside of urban areas are less likely to have any choice at all. . . .

Reduced Choices Have Led to Price Hikes

The evidence evaluated in the report quantifies the lack of competition in the market for local telephone services in California. Many California consumers face a market with only one alternative to their local telephone company—this "choice" is not sufficient to provide consumer protection. Economists refer to this market structure as a duopoly. The report indicates that duopoly markets have not been observed to perform well from the standpoint of encouraging price competition and protecting consumers. The performance of the

Deregulation Before Meaningful Competition Spells Consumer Disaster

It is evident that the Telecommunications Act of 1996 has failed to produce the consumer benefits policy makers promised because competition has failed to take hold across the communications industry. The act's failure is not because, as some have suggested, the Federal Communications Commission (FCC) was overly regulatory in seeking to create conditions ripe for competition. The fundamental problem is that the huge companies that dominate the telephone and cable TV industries prefer mergers and acquisitions to competition. They have refused to open their markets by dragging their feet in allowing competitors to interconnect, refusing to negotiate in good faith, litigating every nook and cranny of the law, and avoiding head-to-head competition like the plague.

Consumers Union, "Lessons from 1996 Telecommunications Act: Deregulation Before Meaningful Competition Spells Consumer Disaster," February 2001. www.consumersunion.org.

duopoly in California's residential telephone service market—an ongoing string of rate increases—indicates another market failure.

As the old saying goes, "the proof of the pudding is in the eating." If market competition is working, why the ongoing stream of price increases? Why have the main rivals to the local telephone company, the cable companies, increased rates following telephone company rate increases? Observed pricing behavior on the part of local telephone companies and their cable rivals does not reveal evidence of price competition.

Rather, pricing reflects the actions of firms that recognize that consumers have little choice, resulting in dramatic rate increases for many California consumers.

In light of these findings, it is clear that the elimination of price caps is failing to protect California consumers. Unless corrective action is taken, consumers will pay prices that reflect the exercise of market power, leading to the undesirable outcomes of excessive prices, undue discrimination, and the unwarranted transfer of income from consumers to the providers of local telephone services.

A Regulatory Framework Is Needed

As the last threads of price protection for basic service rates for most consumers will be removed in early 2011, it is imperative that the CPUC take action to reinstate reasonable price caps for local service rates. As the CPUC's decision also permits, beginning in 2011, geographic de-averaging, i.e., local telephone companies will gain the ability to target specific communities with basic service rate increases, it is imperative that this provision of the CPUC's decision also be reversed. The continuing market power identified in the companion report, combined with local telephone companies' ability to geographically target rate increases, can only increase the harms already experienced by California consumers.

The following actions should be taken:

- It is imperative that the CPUC take action to reinstate reasonable price caps for local service rates. The price caps should, at a minimum, constrain basic rate increases to no more than the rate of inflation.

- The geographic de-averaging provision of the CPUC's decision must also be reversed. The continuing market power identified in the companion report, combined with local telephone companies' ability to geographically target rate increases, can only increase the harms already experienced by California consumers.

- In addition to a price cap on basic rates, [California] LifeLine rate increases should be reversed, and a uniform, affordable, LifeLine rate should be established statewide. The continued affordability of basic telephone service to low-income households is a pressing issue given the economic crisis that is gripping California.

- Finally, the CPUC should more closely monitor market outcomes associated with pricing, service quality, and the delivery of advanced services.

Market forces are failing to deliver the benefits that the telephone companies promised the CPUC as it made its decision to lift price caps. It is time to reestablish an effective regulatory framework that will protect consumers and ensure that high-quality telecommunications services are available to all Californians at reasonable rates.

> "Railroads were freed of much regulation because it was strangling the industry; additional regulation [on shipping] might easily eliminate the small profit margins the roads currently earn."

Deregulation Has Helped the Shipping Industry

Thomas Gale Moore

Thomas Gale Moore is a senior fellow at the Hoover Institution at Stanford University. Between 1985 and 1989 he was a member of President Ronald Reagan's Council of Economic Advisers.

The deregulation of trucking has been a big success, claims Moore in the following viewpoint. Moore points to lower costs per load, improved service quality, more jobs for nonunion workers, an increase in the number of licensed carriers, and significant cost savings for manufacturers as examples of the improvements deregulation has brought to trucking. He suggests that the removal of remaining federal and state regulations could save shippers additional money.

As you read, consider the following questions:

1. What were some of the problems caused by the Interstate Commerce Commission's regulations reducing competition?

2. What impact did deregulation have on trucking rates?

3. What evidence does Moore cite to support his contention that service to small communities has improved under deregulation?

With the establishment of the Interstate Commerce Commission (ICC) to oversee the railroad industry in 1887, the federal government began more than a century of regulating surface freight transportation. . . .

History of Regulation

The federal government nationalized the railroads during World War I, and by the end of the war had provided about $1.5 billion (1919 dollars) in subsidies to the ailing railroads. The major concern after the war was to make the railroads profitable. The Transportation Act of 1920 essentially cartelized [controlled through regulation] the railroad industry and mandated that the Interstate Commerce Commission establish rates to provide a "fair rate of return." . . .

Even during the prosperous 1920s, railroad earnings never reached what the act indicated might be a fair rate of return. New competition from the growing trucking industry presented a major problem for the railroads. With the advent of the Great Depression, earnings plummeted and, for the first time, became negative for the whole railroad industry. In an attempt to improve their profitability, leaders of the railroad industry, together with the ICC, urged Congress to regulate these competitors.

The trucking industry also suffered during the Depression and began to favor allowing the ICC to restrict competition.

With the major spokesmen for a number of large truckers arguing for controls to prevent "cutthroat competition," Congress moved to control motor carriers and inland water carriers.

The Motor Carrier Act of 1935 required new truckers to seek a "certificate of public convenience and necessity" from the ICC. Truckers already operating in 1935 could automatically get certificates, but only if they documented their prior service—and the ICC was extraordinarily restrictive in interpreting proof of service. New trucking companies found it extremely difficult to get certificates. In 1940, Congress extended ICC regulation to include inland water carriers, another competitor of the railroads. Thus, with pipeline regulation, which originated with the Hepburn Act of 1906, the ICC controlled all forms of surface freight transportation (air freight was controlled separately).

From 1940 to 1980, new or expanded authority to transport goods was almost impossible to secure unless an application was completely unopposed. Even if no existing carriers were offering the proposed service, the ICC held that any already certified trucker who expressed a desire to carry the goods should be allowed to do so; new applicants were denied. The effect was to stifle competition from new carriers.

By reducing competition the ICC created a hugely wasteful and inefficient industry. Routes and the products that could be carried over them were narrowly specified. Truckers with authority to carry a product, such as tiles, from one city to another often lacked authority to haul anything on the return trip. Regulation frequently required truckers to go miles out of their way.

During the first three-quarters of the twentieth century, the ICC kept a stranglehold on railroads, preventing them from abandoning unprofitable lines and business. Regulations restricted rates and encouraged price collusion. As a result, by the end of this period many railroads faced bankruptcy, and Congress faced the prospect of having to take over the railroads to keep them operating.

Regulation's Costs

Studies show that regulation increased costs and rates significantly. Not only were rates lower without regulation, but service quality, as judged by shippers, also was better. Products exempt from regulation moved at rates 20–40 percent below those for the same products subject to ICC controls. Regulated rates for carrying cooked poultry, compared with unregulated charges for fresh dressed poultry (a similar product), for example, were nearly 50 percent higher. . . .

In 1962, John Kennedy became the first president to send a message to Congress recommending a reduction in the regulation of surface freight transportation. In November 1975, President Gerald Ford called for legislation to reduce trucking regulation. He followed that proposal by appointing several pro-competition commissioners to the ICC. By the end of 1976, those commissioners were speaking out for a more competitive policy at the ICC, a position rarely articulated in the previous eight decades of transportation regulation.

President Jimmy Carter followed Ford's lead by appointing strong deregulatory advocates and supporting legislation to reduce motor carrier regulation. After a series of ICC rulings that reduced federal oversight of trucking, and after the deregulation of the airline industry, Congress, spurred by the Carter administration, enacted the Motor Carrier Act of 1980. This act limited the ICC's authority over trucking.

Over the last quarter of a century, Congress has sharply curtailed regulation of transportation, starting with the Railroad Revitalization and Regulatory Reform Act of 1976 (the 4-R Act), the Motor Carrier Act of 1980, the Household Goods [Transportation] Act of 1980, the Staggers Rail Act of 1980, the Bus Regulatory Reform Act of 1982, the Surface Freight

Forwarder Deregulation Act of 1986, the Negotiated Rates Act of 1993, the Trucking Industry Regulatory Reform Act of 1994, and the ICC Termination Act of 1995. Those acts deregulated successively, either totally or in large part, trucking, railroads, bus service, and freight forwarders, and lifted most of the remaining motor carrier restrictions, including those imposed by the states.

Deregulation of motor carriers became complete—except for household movers—at the end of 1995 with the ICC Termination Act of 1995, which also established the Surface Transportation Board [STB] as part of the Department of Transportation to continue to monitor the railroad industry. The act transferred truck licensing, mainly for safety purposes, to the Federal Highway Administration. At that time, the federal government also preempted state regulation of trucking, eliminating the last controls over price and service in the motor carrier industry. It eliminated the need for motor carriers to file rates and authorized truckers to carry goods wherever they wanted to serve. Railroads were given more freedom to price, except when "captured shippers" could show that they faced a single carrier without significant alternatives.

The Success of Deregulation

Deregulation has worked well. Between 1977, the year before the ICC started to decontrol the industry, and 1982, rates for truckload-size shipments fell by about 25 percent in inflation-adjusted terms. The General Accounting Office [currently the Government Accountability Office] found that rates charged by LTL (less-than-truckload) carriers had fallen by as much as 10–20 percent, with some shippers reporting declines of as much as 40 percent. Revenue per truckload-ton fell by 22 percent from 1979 to 1986. A survey of shippers indicates that they believe service quality improved as well. Some 77 percent of surveyed shippers favored deregulation of trucking. Ship-

---

The Shipping Industry's Volume and Revenue Shares, 2003

Mode	Share of Tons (%)	Share of Revenue (%)
Trucks	68.9	86.9
Rail	12.9	5.1
Intermodal	0.9	1.1
Air	0.1	1.9
Water	7.7	1.1
Pipeline	9.4	3.9

TAKEN FROM: American Trucking Association, April 28, 2004/Thomas Gale Moore, "Surface Freight Transportation Deregulation," *The Concise Encyclopedia of Economics*, 2008.

---

pers reported that carriers were much more willing to negotiate rates and services than they had been prior to deregulation.

The Surface Transportation Board reports that railroad rates fell by 45 percent in inflation-adjusted dollars from 1984 to 1999. The demise of the ICC at the end of 1994 eliminated many of the statistics collected on the motor carrier industry. However, limited data show that revenue per ton-miles, adjusted for inflation, continued to decline, falling by 29 percent from 1990 to 1999. How much of this is due to deregulation and how much might be attributed to technological improvements, improvement in roads, and other factors is difficult to determine.

In arguing against deregulation, the American Trucking Association predicted that service would decline and that small communities would find it harder to get any service at all. In fact, service to small communities improved, and shippers' complaints against truckers declined. The ICC reported that, in 1975 and 1976, it handled 340 and 390 complaints, respectively; in 1980, it dealt with only 23 cases, and in 1981, with just 40.

Deregulation has also made it easier for nonunion workers to get jobs in the trucking industry. This new competition has sharply eroded the strength of the drivers' union, the International Brotherhood of Teamsters. Before deregulation, ICC-regulated truckers paid unionized workers about 50 percent more than comparable workers in other industries. In 1997, the median wage for union and nonunion drivers was $43,165 and $35,551, respectively, while the median wage in the United States for that year was only $25,598. Thus, union drivers still commanded a premium of roughly 21 percent, but even non-union drivers make more than the wage earned by half the labor force. The number of unionized workers in the industry has fallen considerably, with only 13 percent of the drivers and warehouse workers belonging to the union in 2002, down from around 60 percent in the late 1970s.

The number of new firms has increased dramatically. In 2004, the American Trucking Association, the largest trade association for the motor carrier industry, reported having nearly thirty-eight thousand members, considerably more than double the number licensed by the ICC in 1978. While the ICC used to license carriers for specific routes, now all carriers can go wherever their business takes them. The value of operating rights granted by the ICC, worth hundreds of thousands of dollars when such authority was almost impossible to secure, has plummeted to zero now that operating rights are easily obtained.

Intermodal carriage surged sharply from 1981 to 1986, but has since leveled off. The ability of railroads and truckers to develop an extensive trailer-on-flatcar network is a direct result of the Motor Carrier Act of 1980 and the Staggers [Rail] Act (1980), which partially freed the railroads. . . .

One of the economy's major gains from trucking deregulation has been the substantial drop in the cost of holding and maintaining inventories. Since truckers are better able to offer on-time delivery and more flexible service, manufacturers can order components just in time to be used, and retailers can have them just in time to be sold. The Department of Transportation estimated that the gains to consumers were $15.8 billion (in 1990 dollars). This does not include the annual benefits to industry of reduced inventories, which have been estimated to be as high as $100 billion.

Some Issues Still Need Attention

With the virtually total deregulation of motor carriers—household movers must still file rates—railroads alone remain under control. For certain shipments, railroad pricing is still regulated. If the railroad has a shipper who has no good alternative means of moving his product, the railroad cannot charge more than 180 percent of variable costs. In those "captive shipper" cases, the shipper can bring a case before the STB asking the board to force the railroad to lower its charges. The STB must then estimate variable costs and determine whether the rates are unreasonable. Coal and grain companies have exploited this provision to gain lower rates. Thus, the government forces the railroads to subsidize coal and grain companies at the expense of other shippers, the railroads' stockholders, and investments in maintenance and new facilities. Captive shippers represent about 20 percent of the railroad business and do face higher rates, but the cost to the economy is very small and the gain from using the market much greater. . . .

The Congress should also refrain from adding more regulation. Some shippers and legislators have been urging the government to require "open access"—that is, requiring one railroad that has the only tracks to a particular shipper to let other railroads service that customer over its tracks. The other proposal is to require railroads to quote rates to any two points on their lines ("bottleneck rates"). Both of these steps would force the STB to regulate rates and determine costs of service, a step backward in freeing the railroads from government controls. Railroads were freed of much regulation because it was strangling the industry; additional regulation might easily eliminate the small profit margins the roads currently earn, leading to reduced maintenance, bankruptcies, or both.

Economists Agree on Deregulation of Transportation

The writings of economists have driven the deregulation of airlines, motor carriers, and railroads. Right from the beginning of trucking regulation, economists questioned the need and desirability of government control over rates and service. Research showed how costly those regulations were to the economy. In a 1973 study done for a Brookings Institution conference, this author estimated that the costs imposed on the U.S. economy by ICC regulation were somewhere between $3.8 and $8.9 billion yearly, in 1968 dollars. In 1974, President Ford organized an economic summit meeting dealing with inflation, to which he called some of the leading economists in the country. Although many people believe that economists never agree, twenty-three economists signed a statement at that meeting recommending deregulation of transportation. The result has been all that economists predicted.

> "We got a system that shifts business costs onto the public and onto truck drivers, suppresses private investment in innovation and new technology, and forces trucking companies into competing by cutting corners."

Deregulation Has Harmed the Shipping Industry

David Bensman

David Bensman is a professor of labor studies and employment relations at Rutgers University. He is the coauthor of Rusted Dreams: Hard Times in a Steel Community.

Deregulation has crippled the U.S. trucking industry, particularly in contrast to efficient systems being employed in Europe, according to Bensman in the following viewpoint. A lack of federal regulations has resulted in lower wages for drivers, lack of attention to emission controls, outdated trucks, and inefficient logistics. Although several states have stepped into the breach to address environmental and labor issues, federal regulation is needed to improve trucking, the author contends.

As you read, consider the following questions:

1. According to Bensman, why aren't trucks made to comply with the Environmental Protection Agency's standards?

2. Why has FedEx been fined by the Internal Revenue Service for its policies toward its drivers?

3. What are some of the actions taking place in California to address abuses in the trucking industry?

Rotterdam, Europe's largest port, is a marvel of efficiency. More than 7,000 container ships visit its docks annually, most stopping for barely more than a day. New terminal facilities, built on landfill where the river meets the sea, handle 10 million containers with a minimum of congestion and pollution.

The Rotterdam Model

The freight—Chinese clothing and electronics, American pharmaceuticals, Spanish automobiles—seamlessly flows to warehouses, distribution centers, rail yards, and barges surrounding the port, on time and on schedule. The tightly integrated freight-movement system at the port makes it possible to operate a just-in-time logistics system in which goods arrive at their destination 15 minutes before they are moved to their next spot on the supply chain. This allows shippers to operate with minimal inventory, a must on a continent where most retail shops have minimal space to store goods. Lean logistics means lower interest costs on merchandise, lower insurance costs, less theft, and less need to discount unsold goods.

By comparison, American ports and the logistics and distribution systems they feed are old world. Trucks clog the overwhelmed highways and roads leading to the ports. Thick diesel pollution fouls the air not only in the ports and neighboring communities but in inland warehouse districts under siege from container trucks and freight trains. Stacks of containers form walls around residential communities. Traffic congestion slows commuting time and wastes fuel. Rates of asthma as well as lung and heart disease are climbing. And just-in-time delivery is impossible in a system where old, worn-out container trucks, without digital communication, spend half their days waiting.

Port trucking—the industry segment that carries containers to and from ports, warehouses, and railroad yards—is one of the most extreme cases of abuse. Competition for work is intense. Instead of a computerized system advising a driver to pick up a container at a designated loading dock at a particular time, drivers sit and wait, engines on. Since the drivers bear the costs, there is no incentive for trucking companies to modernize. Freight rates paid to drivers are so low that the median age of the trucks driven by the nation's 70,000 port truckers exceeds 11 years. How is this possible when the Environmental Protection Agency [EPA] adopted diesel engine standards in 2001 that required trucks to meet stringent standards for emissions by 2007? Simple—the EPA bowed to the reality that the U.S. has chosen a low-road freight transport policy and grandfathered all used trucks that were on the road when the standards went into effect. By contrast, Rotterdam's trucks—indeed all trucks in Holland, are tested regularly to ensure compliance with strict emission standards. Nearly all the trucks working in Rotterdam's just-in-time logistics system are owned by trucking companies that employ their drivers, and all the trucks are less than five years old.

U.S. Trucking Takes Advantage of Drivers

Americans chose this low road for freight movement in 1980, when Congress deregulated the trucking industry, disbanding the Interstate Commerce Commission. Advocates ranging from consumer advocate Ralph Nader and Sen. Ted Kennedy to the nation's retailers and the agricultural freight-hauling industry predicted that deregulation would bring market competition, lower rates, and economic growth. Instead, we got a system that shifts business costs onto the public and onto truck drivers, suppresses private investment in innovation and new technology, and forces trucking companies into competing by cutting corners, like carrying overweight containers, or depriving drivers of fuel surcharges.

The rise in drivers misclassified as "independent contractors" is symptomatic of the low road on which American freight transport policy has been stuck for more than a quarter-century. Whereas trucking was once a stable job, with industrial wages and benefits, deregulation meant that hundreds of thousands of truck drivers had to give up their employment contracts, union representation, and the protection of labor legislation. Today these owner-operators must provide their own trucks, pay for their own employment taxes, maintain their equipment, buy fuel and insurance, and directly bear the risk of economic downturns, health emergencies, and equipment failures. Twelve-hour days without compensation for overtime have become the norm. Drivers skimp on maintenance, which causes their engines to emit excessive cancer-causing diesel particulates. An owner-operator may gross around $80,000, minus costs averaging $52,000, and take home perhaps $28,000 before taxes. All the risks are the driver's.

A classic case is FedEx Ground operations. FedEx saves money and resists unionization by disguising its drivers as contractors or temps—something that is illegal under labor law. A California court found (in *Estrada v. FedEx Ground*) that delivery drivers were employees in everything but name. They were made to buy or lease trucks that met company specifications, were required to pay for the company logo to be painted on their trucks, and were dressed in company uniforms, down to the color of their socks and shoes. They made pickups and deliveries on routes assigned by the company, were barred from using their trucks to haul loads for other companies, and had to park their trucks in company-assigned spaces. The court found that FedEx Ground misclassified its drivers as independent contractors as an illegal means to avoid paying state unemployment insurance and workers' compensation insurance. It levied a $17.6 million fine against the company. A class action suit consolidating suits against FedEx Ground's misclassification is supposed to be heard in northern Indiana in the fall [2009]. In 2007, the Internal Revenue Service fined FedEx $319 million for its misclassification of workers.

FedEx also used its political muscle to change which labor law it is subject to, in order to deter unionization. In 1996, as Congress cleared the decks for a summer recess, FedEx lobbyists had friendly legislators insert into a transportation bill two words—"express carrier"—which had the effect of excluding the employees of FedEx from coverage by the National Labor Relations Act (NLRA). Instead, the revised bill put these workers in the same category as airline and railroad workers, who are covered by the provisions of the Railway Labor Act. That act, unlike the NLRA, requires systemwide bargaining units.

Thus, when Massachusetts FedEx employees voted for union representation by the International Brotherhood of Teamsters in an election conducted by the National Labor Relations Board, a federal district court panel voided the election on the grounds that FedEx employees, unlike the employees of other express delivery companies, were governed by the Railway Labor Act. That meant they could not organize one work center at a time. In May, the House of Representatives voted to end FedEx's exemption from the NLRA. In retaliation, the company threatened to cancel its orders for new planes from Boeing, jeopardizing the [Barack] Obama administration's recovery plans. Soon thereafter, FedEx announced a multimillion-dollar advertising campaign, attacking the House vote as a "bailout" of rival UPS, which is largely unionized. The legislation, part of an omnibus transportation bill, is still pending.

Federal Intervention Is Needed

Is there any hope that the Obama administration and Congress will place America's freight-transit system back on the high road with enforceable environmental and labor standards making possible modern, just-in-time logistics? There are some positive indications. As a senator, Barack Obama sponsored legislation aimed at ending misclassification of independent contractors who are employees in everything but name. As a presidential candidate, he endorsed the Port of Los Angeles's Clean Truck Program, championed by environmental groups and the Change to Win Federation. The program sets emissions standards for trucks and requires companies to classify their drivers as employees. And the House's transportation bill, shepherded by Transportation Committee Chair James Oberstar of Minnesota, embraces the vision of a freight-transport system with cleaner fuel, more modern freight-hauling equipment, and better infrastructure. Legislation aimed at tightening the rules against misclassification of employees is pending (House Bill 09-1310), and there is much that the administration could do with better enforcement of existing laws.

But it won't be easy. In July, Transportation Secretary Ray LaHood announced that the administration would support delaying consideration of the House bill's ambitious transportation policy reform in order to keep Congress focused on health care and energy legislation. The trucking industry has tied up the Los Angeles reform program in court. On April 28, 2009, Christina A. Snyder, U.S. District Judge of the Central District of California, issued a preliminary injunction against those parts of the Los Angeles and Long Beach plans that are not directly related to safety, on the grounds that the

Federal Aviation Administration [Authorization] Act of 1994 preempts local regulations. She did permit the Los Angeles Harbor Commission to phase out the oldest trucks on safety grounds. A full hearing won't begin until December. The delay could cripple a plan that has already succeeded in forcing hundreds of the worst trucks to be retired and induced companies to put almost 5,000 new trucks on the road.

Furthermore, because of the ambiguities in the federal legislation governing classification of employees and independent contractors, there is no guarantee that the FedEx Ground class action suit set to open this fall will eliminate misclassification. Instead, it could uphold independent contracting as standard practice in the industry.

All current proposals to move freight transport off the low road stop short of establishing the sort of regulatory authority that disappeared when the Interstate Commerce Commission was eliminated in 1980. Since then, there has been no effective authority ensuring that containers are not overweight, that leasing agreements conform to the law, and that the rigs are safe.

In the absence of decisive federal leadership, states and cities have been at the forefront, motivated by a desire to find new revenue sources as well as to eliminate diesel pollution. California, suffering from both budget distress and lethal smog, is in the lead. In addition to the efforts by the Los Angeles Harbor Commission to regularize port trucking, the state attorney general's office has been looking into misclassification of port truckers at the ports of Los Angeles and Long Beach since October 2008. In July, an official with the California attorney general's office reported that five cases have been filed, but investigators have looked at dozens of companies because the problem is "pervasive," and more suits will be filed soon as a part of the ongoing crackdown. Taking their cue from California, attorneys general from eight states announced in June that they would work together to investigate FedEx Ground's classification of its drivers as "independent contractors."

"State and local governments in Ohio are being cheated out of hundreds of millions of dollars each year as a result of employee misclassification," said Attorney General Richard Cordray of Ohio. "We are committed to aggressively pursuing these misclassification cases to level the playing field for businesses that play by the rules and to protect Ohio's workers."

While the Los Angeles Harbor Commission's Clean Air [Action] Plan, the California attorney general's investigation, the *Estrada* decision, and the eight attorneys general's joint investigation of FedEx Ground are all promising signs that cities and states are recognizing their stake in moving American freight transport onto the high road, federal leadership is necessary. The aviation and transportation bill points the way, with its emphasis on alternative fuels, expanding rail capacity, modernizing infrastructure, reducing diesel emissions, and recognizing workers' rights to organize under the NLRA. More leadership is necessary if America's freight-movement system is ever to change to a lean logistics model like the one that already exists in Rotterdam.

Periodical Bibliography

The following articles have been selected to supplement the diverse views presented in this chapter.

Jack Casazza	"Electrical Power Deregulation—A Bad Idea?" *IEEE-USA Today's Engineer Online*, May 2005. www.todaysengineer.org.
Braden Cox and Fred L. Smith Jr.	"Airline Deregulation," Competitive Enterprise Institute, August 18, 2008. http://cei.org.
Thomas A. Fogarty and Edward Iwata	"Energy Deregulation: Is It Friend or Enemy?" *USA Today*, May 15, 2002.
David Cay Johnston	"A New Push to Regulate Power Costs," *New York Times*, September 4, 2007.
Eric Lipton and Gardiner Harris	"In Turnaround, Industries Seek U.S. Regulations," *New York Times*, September 16, 2007.
Micheline Maynard	"Did Ending Regulation Help Fliers?" *New York Times*, April 17, 2008.
Elizabeth Souder and Eric Torbenson	"Texas Electricity Deregulation Opinions All Over the Grid in Industry Panel," *Dallas Morning News*, February 28, 2010.
Transport Workers Solidarity Committee	"Flying Blind: Airline Deregulation, 30 Years Later," April 2, 2010. http://transportworkers.org.
Matt Welch	"Fly the Frugal Skies," *Reason*, January 2005.

CHAPTER 4

How Has Deregulation Affected the Global Economy?

Chapter Preface

Why was the recent financial crisis a global one? Why did a downturn in the U.S. housing market create a ripple effect around the world—bringing the economies of Iceland and Greece, for instance, to their knees? The short answer is due to the interconnectedness of the global economy. An influential force in regulating the global economy is the World Trade Organization (WTO), with a membership of 153 nations and a purpose to promote free and open trading among nations resulting in economic growth. A subject of international debate is what role, if any, the policies of the World Trade Organization had in creating or spreading the financial crisis.

In 1999, the World Trade Organization's Financial Services Agreement became law and broke down previous rules against intercountry trade in currency and financial derivatives.[1] This opened a global market for U.S. mortgage-backed securities.[2] When many of the underlying assets in these securities proved to be toxic, the impact was felt worldwide. According to Greg Palast, in the *Nation* on December 2, 2009,

> In 1999 the international trade in equity derivatives and credit default swaps[3] was too rare to track. But thanks to WTO treaty terms negotiated by Timothy Geithner, then assistant treasury secretary for international affairs, cross-border trade in swaps and derivatives would grow to a $115 trillion business by 2008, the year of Citigroup's near collapse and government bailout.

For its part, the World Trade Organization denies any complicity in the events that resulted in the global economic crisis. WTO Director-General Pascal Lamy, in an interview with Palast on November 30, 2009, stated:

The cause of the crisis is not openness [free trade] ... the cause of the crisis is a lack of proper regulation. ... A sick cow in today's world doesn't cross borders, because this is regulated. Financial activities are exactly the same. Except that, in this case, toxic financial products could cross borders without any problem.

In a speech to the International Chamber of Commerce on February 3, 2009, Lamy argued that an overreaction creating increased regulation could curtail global trade and impede economic growth:

We all risk seeing trade and the WTO lumped together with the elements of the Washington [D.C.] consensus which many believe to have failed—with de-regulation and privatisations. And it is now that we risk throwing the baby out with the bath water. This is why now more than ever it is time to stress the value of trade as a multiplier of growth and the value of the multilateral trading system, with its 60 years of global regulation, as an insurance policy against protectionism.

While the role the WTO played in the global crisis is subject to debate, it is undeniable that different countries were affected in different ways. China and Canada came through the crisis with relatively robust economies, while countries such as Iceland and Greece nearly collapsed. The role that deregulation played in various countries is the subject of debate among the commentators and analysts in the following chapter.

Notes

1. Derivatives have no underlying financial worth but are instead financial products whose worth is based on changes in the value of the underlying asset. Underlying assets usually consist of stocks or groupings of stocks in an index, a specific financial event, interest rates, or commodities. Participants in derivatives are essentially wagering that the as-

set will either grow or decline, and will be paid, or lose their investment, based on the behavior of the asset.

2. A mortgage-backed security (MBS) represents an investor's interest in a pool of mortgage loans. These securities are created when a financial institution buys mortgages from a primary lender, sells them to various investors—spreading the risk—and uses the monthly mortgage payments to compensate investors.

3. A credit default swap (CDS) is a transaction where the buyer of a bond or loan makes payments to the seller, who guarantees the creditworthiness of the product. The buyer receives a payment from the seller if the product goes into default.

> *"It would be a mistake to underestimate the determination of G-20 leaders to reshape the financial services industry."*

The G-20 Is Advancing Global Regulatory Reform

Mark Carney

Mark Carney is governor of the Bank of Canada.

In the following viewpoint, Carney is optimistic that the reforms spearheaded by the G-20, a forum of financial leaders from twenty countries, will stabilize global financial markets. He describes the two issues being addressed by the G-20 reforms: making individual banks stronger and making financial markets less interdependent. To make banks stronger, he recommends higher capital requirements, decreasing the amount of debt banks can take on, and improvements in risk management. In order to reduce systemic risk, any future institutional failures need to be borne by the institutions themselves, not by taxpayers, he maintains.

As you read, consider the following questions:

1. What does the author state to be the objective of the G-20 financial reforms?

Mark Carney, "Reforming the Global Financial System," *BIS Review*, vol. 133, October 26, 2009, pp. 1–4, 6. © 2009 Bank for International Settlements ("BIS"). Reproduced by permission of the Bank of Canada.

2. According to the author, how do compensation practices relate to the need to increase the capital requirements of banks?

3. The author states that meaningful financial reform won't happen without a change in attitude among bankers. What are some of the examples he gives of this?

It is a pleasure to be here at this year's Rendez-vous avec l'Autorité des marchés financiers (AMF).

After briefly reviewing the current macrofinancial environment, I intend to concentrate on the G-20 reform agenda. The financial crisis has cost tens of millions of jobs and trillions of dollars in foregone output. Its aftershocks will persist for years. To prevent an even more severe outcome, monetary and fiscal policies have been stretched to their very limits.

In this context, it would be a mistake to underestimate the determination of G-20 leaders to reshape the financial services industry. Last month in Pittsburgh, the leaders of the G-20 endorsed a comprehensive agenda, whose implementation is just beginning. As I will highlight during my remarks, Canada intends to use its presidency of the G-7 next year to advance some of the most important priorities.

Current Outlook

Recent indicators point to the start of a global recovery. Economic and financial developments have been somewhat more favourable than the Bank had expected in July, although significant fragilities remain. In Canada, as expected, a recovery in economic activity is also under way, following three consecutive quarters of sharp contraction. This resumption of growth is supported by monetary and fiscal stimulus, increased household wealth, improving financial conditions, higher commodity prices, and stronger business and consumer confidence.

However, heightened volatility and persistent strength in the Canadian dollar are working to slow growth and subdue inflation pressures. The current strength in the dollar is expected, over time, to more than fully offset the favourable developments since July.

Given all these factors, the Bank now projects that, relative to our July *Monetary Policy Report*, the composition of aggregate demand will shift further towards final domestic demand and away from net exports. We now expect growth to average slightly lower over the balance of the projection period. The Bank projects that the Canadian economy will contract by 2.4 per cent this year and then grow by 3.0 per cent in 2010 and 3.3 per cent in 2011. This projected recovery will be somewhat more modest than the average of previous cycles.

Total CPI inflation declined to a trough of -0.9 per cent in the third quarter, reflecting large year-on-year drops in energy prices. Total CPI inflation should rise to 1.0 per cent this quarter, while the core rate of inflation is projected to reach its trough of 1.4 per cent during the same period. Owing to the substantial excess supply that has emerged in the economy, the Bank expects both core and total inflation to return to the 2 per cent target in the third quarter of 2011, one quarter later than we projected in July.

The main upside risks to inflation relate to the possibility of a stronger-than-anticipated recovery in the global economy and more robust Canadian domestic demand.

On the downside, the global recovery could be even more protracted than projected. In addition, a stronger-than-assumed Canadian dollar, driven by global portfolio movements out of U.S.-dollar assets, could act as a significant further drag on growth and put additional downward pressure on inflation.

On Tuesday, the Bank reaffirmed its conditional commitment to maintain its target for the overnight rate at the effective lower bound of ¼ per cent until the end of June 2010 in order to achieve the inflation target. The Bank retains considerable flexibility in the conduct of monetary policy at low interest rates, consistent with the framework that we outlined in the April MPR.

As I said last week, our focus in the conduct of monetary policy is on achieving the 2 per cent inflation target. The exchange rate should be seen in this context. It is an important relative price, which the Bank monitors closely. What ultimately matters is the exchange rate's impact in conjunction with all other domestic and foreign factors on aggregate demand and inflation in Canada. To put it simply, the Bank looks at everything through the prism of achieving our inflation target.

Current Macrofinancial Environment

As many of you have no doubt noticed, it is currently a very constructive environment for financial institutions. Flow trading and market making have become more attractive and intermediation spreads have increased. Underwriting fees have recovered along with the capital markets; and there are very early signs that an appetite for mergers and acquisitions has returned. Banks are once again being compensated for their basic businesses of providing liquidity and credit. Interestingly, despite the fall in measured volatility, industry VaR, while down from the peak earlier this year, is still above pre-Lehman levels.

What is perhaps less evident is that these returns are largely the product of public policy. While medium-term challenges clearly remain, tail risk has been removed from the economic outlook. The very low policy interest rates and greater-than-usual clarity on policy paths are encouraging investors to return to the markets and to take on greater risk.

Direct support to the industry has been breathtaking, with some industrialized countries committing a remarkable 25 per cent of GDP to support their financial sectors. In effect, there was wartime spending on peacetime calamity. The G-7 commitments of last October temporarily eliminated counterparty risk for major institutions. When this support was combined with an intense flight to quality, large financial institutions benefited disproportionately.

Even in Canada, public funding has been considerable. The $65 billion in Insured Mortgage Purchase Program (IMPP) funding for banks represents 4.3 per cent of GDP. Bank of Canada extraordinary liquidity facilities have been smaller than elsewhere but they still peaked at 3 per cent of GDP. While government guarantees have not been used, it is noteworthy that Canadian bank term funding is running at less than 30 per cent of normal levels, largely as a result of the use of IMPP and the Bank's facilities.

Initially, the crisis has also had a major impact on the competitive environment for financial institutions. Competition globally has been substantially reduced through the combination of the failure of institutions, a decline in cross-border banking and, most importantly, the collapse of most of the shadow banking system. The reduced competitive dynamics could persist for some time, allowing the core of the financial sector to build sufficient capital for the future. Banks around the world would be well advised to take this opportunity to do so.

The G-20 Reform Agenda

The fundamental objective of the G-20 reforms is to create a resilient, global financial system that efficiently supports worldwide economic growth. The system must be robust to shocks, dampening rather than amplifying their impact on the real economy.

The Bank of Canada strongly believes that our destination should be one where financial institutions and markets play critical—and complementary—roles to support long-term economic prosperity. The financial system will be more stable if market infrastructure is substantially improved, products are more standardized and transparent, and banks are adequately capitalized to fulfill their market-making and credit intermediation roles. Market forces should be left to determine the relative sizes and boundaries of the banking and market sectors. In doing so, markets can discipline banks by furnishing necessary competition.

There are two main approaches to reform:

- First, protect the banks from the economic cycle; in other words, make each bank, individually, more resilient.

- Second, protect the cycle from the banks; that is, make the system as a whole more resilient.

Both are necessary.

Protecting the Banks from the Cycle

In effect, the objective of the first approach is to create more resilient institutions. This will require more capital, higher liquidity, and better risk management.

In early September, my colleagues and I on the oversight body of the Basel Committee on Banking Supervision (BCBS) met to review a comprehensive set of measures to strengthen the regulation, supervision, and risk management of the banking sector. We agreed on new standards for banking regulation and supervision, which should help reduce the probability and severity of economic and financial stress. These standards were endorsed by G-20 leaders in Pittsburgh.

Specifically, to protect banks from the cycle, we agreed to:

- Raise the quality, consistency, and transparency of the Tier 1 capital base. Going forward, the predominant form of Tier 1 capital must consist of common shares and retained earnings. Moreover, deductions and prudential filters (such as goodwill and other intangibles, investments in own shares, deferred tax assets, etc.) will be harmonized internationally and generally applied at the level of common equity. Finally, all components of the capital base will be fully disclosed.

- Introduce a leverage ratio as a supplementary measure of capital adequacy to the Basel II risk-based framework. To ensure comparability, the details of the leverage ratio will be harmonised internationally, fully adjusting for differences in accounting (such as netting).

These two measures will make international bank capital regulation look more like the existing capital regulations overseen by Canada's Office of the Superintendent of Financial Institutions (OSFI). Other initiatives will be new, even to Canada:[1]

- Introduce a framework for countercyclical capital buffers above the minimum requirement. The Bank of Canada is working closely with OSFI and our international counterparts on proposed elements of this framework.

- Create a minimum global standard for funding liquidity that includes requirement for a stressed liquidity-coverage ratio, underpinned by a longer-term structural liquidity ratio. As in other areas, standard setters will need to take a comprehensive approach.

1. A system-wide, or macroprudential, approach is the shared responsibility of the Department of Finance and all of the federal financial regulatory authorities, including, of course, the Bank of Canada, the Office of the Superintendent of Financial Institutions, and the Canada Deposit Insurance Corporation. Ultimately, it is the Minister of Finance who is responsible for the sound stewardship of the financial system.

Central banks have real concerns about ratchet effects (large buffers are built beyond the standard), particularly in light of the inherent procyclicality of liquidity (i.e., institutions want more liquidity in bad times so "buffers" cannot be drawn upon).

One potential mitigant would be to ensure that there is a broad range of securities that are liquid in all states of the world. That is tougher than it sounds as anyone who tried to repo quasi-sovereigns throughout the last year knows. I will address some potential solutions to this problem momentarily.

The Bank strongly believes that the standard should not bind in times of systemic crises.

The Basel Committee will issue specific, concrete proposals on these measures by the end of this year. It will carry out an impact assessment in the first half of next year, and calibrate the new requirements by the end of 2010. Implementation will be timed to ensure that the phase-in of these new measures does not impede the recovery of the real economy.

Protecting the Cycle from the Banks

Protecting the cycle from the banks requires building a system that can withstand the failure of any single financial institution and is buttressed by resilient markets. Today, after a series of extraordinary but necessary measures to keep the system functioning, we are awash in moral hazard. If left unchecked, this will distort private behaviour and inflate public costs.

As a consequence, there is a firm conviction among policy makers that losses endured in future crises must be borne by the institutions themselves. This means management, shareholders and creditors, rather than taxpayers. This cannot be accomplished overnight. On the contrary, it is a long-term objective that should consistently guide policy choices now and in the future. The following four measures are designed to create a system in which individual financial institutions are less important and markets more important:

- As is the case in Canada, all regulators should institute staged intervention regimes[2] to detect problems early.

- Banks themselves should develop "living wills," or plans to unwind in an orderly fashion if they were to fail. If this process results in simpler organizations, so be it. At a minimum, the exercise will underscore the shared responsibility for financial stability and improve regulators' understanding of firms' business models.

- The Basel oversight committee agreed to "reduce the systemic risk associated with the resolution of cross-border banks." Closing down a multinational institution is a horrifically difficult challenge, but without progress in this area, the efficiency of the global system will likely decline, perhaps significantly. For example, viable cross-border resolution is the key to ensure that a financial institution's liquidity continues to be optimally distributed across its international operations.

- Finally, the Bank of Canada believes that continuously open markets are essential for a system to be robust to failure. The crisis was clearly exacerbated by the seizure of interbank and repo markets. Good collateral became unfinanceable overnight, firms failed, risk aversion skyrocketed, and the global economy plummeted.

Promising avenues to break such (il)liquidity spirals in funding markets include:

- Clearing houses for repo

- Through-the-cycle margining requirements

2. OSFI has developed Guide to Intervention for federally-regulated financial institutions that provide a framework for responding effectively to circumstances that could undermine the financial viability of an institution. It is based on a graduated and progressive set of responses or stages, depending on the institution's situation and degree of weakness perceived. Further information on the staging process can be found at www.osfi-bsif.gc.ca/app/DocRepository/1/eng/practices/supervisory/Guide_Int_e.pdf.

- Standardizing products

- Ensuring that accounting rules permit effective netting

- Adapting central bank liquidity facilities as necessary

In a similar vein, current efforts to transfer settlement of many over-the-counter derivatives onto clearing houses and potentially the trading of some of them onto exchanges, such as the Montreal Exchange, have the potential to reduce bilateral counterparty risk, increase liquidity, and enhance transparency. As a testament to the seriousness of this initiative, the G-7—where the vast majority of such transactions occur—has made this a top priority for implementation next year. The Bank of Canada is working with our partners, including the AMF and the federal Department of Finance, to develop a Canadian approach.

Globally, substantial progress has been made in recent months—more than two-thirds of credit default swaps (CDS) and three-quarters of interest rate swaps (IRS) are now eligible for clearing houses. Of course, there is much more work to be done as actual volumes are still a fraction of these levels.

For such initiatives to be fully successful, regulatory capital requirements should reinforce incentives to process standardized products centrally. That is, trading in standardized products should be capital advantaged and limited basis risk should not result in punitive capital charges. Bespoke transactions will continue to have their place, but should be subject to higher capital requirements so that incentives are appropriately aligned.

Securitization Needs to Be Made More Sustainable

A more resilient financial system will require a return of private-label securitization. When properly structured, securitization can diversify risk, provide competitive discipline on banks and lower borrowing costs for individuals and businesses. Much more must be done to ensure that these objectives can be achieved.

Securitization has been slow to come back for two reasons. First, some core buyers of senior tranches (structured investment vehicles, Canadian non-bank asset-backed commercial paper (ABCP), balance sheets of large banks) will not return. This alone will shrink the market substantially. Some of this shortfall in financing capacity will be replaced over time with on-balance sheet credit risk, though the prospect of leverage ratios will limit future buying by banks of senior tranches.

Second, the crisis laid bare important structural deficiencies, such as the woefully inadequate disclosure on securitized products. Transparency should be improved so that risk can be identified more effectively and priced more efficiently. For example, the Bank of Canada used its collateral policy to improve the disclosure of bank-sponsored ABCP, creating a standard that should become commonplace. More generally, we advocate publication of models and data underlying securities to move securitization from "black box" to "open source." There are also a host of initiatives for underwriters to have skin in the game (keep similar products or first loss).

The Bank is working with government and industry players to explore the effectiveness of these and other alternatives.

An Integrated Approach to Return Risk to the Private Sector

The financial panic required a bold response. While absolutely necessary, the response has profoundly shifted risk from the private to the public sector. The expedient should not become permanent. Risks must be returned to and, borne by, the private sector. However, this can only happen if banks are resilient and if markets are built on solid foundations.

This will require a set of reforms that are internally consistent and mutually reinforcing. Examples just mentioned include clearing houses for CDS and Basel II treatment of basis risk or new liquidity requirements and the development of continuously open funding markets to aid in liquidity options. Reforms cannot be developed and introduced in a piecemeal fashion; the entire package must be integrated.

Similarly, banks should take an integrated approach to how they deploy their current earnings. In this regard, it may be wise to consider that both the Basel Committee and the G-20 are stressing capital conservation during the transition to a new capital regime. The compensation debate should be seen in this context. Current bumper profits can compensate employees, be returned to shareholders, or increase capital. The clear priority of the public sector is the recapitalization of the financial system to expand credit formation. The transition timetable for a new capital regime referenced at the start of my remarks is in part designed to take advantage of current higher retained earnings. The industry should be in no doubt that capital requirements are going up. Those who prefund will be in the best possible position over the medium term.

Moreover, we all agree that bonuses should be tied to long-term performance. In their communiqué, the G-20 leaders urged firms to implement sound compensation practices immediately. The current windfall, dependent as it is on the strongest of safety nets . . . sits uneasily with that principle. Do firms really have a good handle on their medium-term profitability, given the profound regulatory and economic changes on the horizon?

Conclusion: Working Together for Common Solutions

To conclude, the financial system must transition from its self-appointed role as the apex of economic activity to once again be the servant of the real economy. Stronger institutions and a system that can withstand failure are necessary conditions. But full realization of this objective also requires a change in attitude.

The Bank of Canada has a strong preference for principles-based regulation and reliance on the judgment of people, rather than blind faith in the security blanket of excess capital. But this approach requires a sensitivity from the industry, which has been absent in recent months. Relief is in danger of giving way to hubris.

Financial institutions need to demonstrate an awareness of their broader responsibilities. Financiers should ask themselves every day how their activities affect systemic risk? And what are they doing to promote economic growth?

As a colleague said during the crisis, there are no atheists in foxholes, and there are no ideologues in financial crises. Policy makers had to do many unpalatable things to save the economy from the financial system—a financial system that begged for mercy.

We will not remind market participants of the many oaths they swore a year ago; nor do we expect scores of financiers to join religious orders. However, we do expect those fevered battlefield vows to be respected through daily peacetime concern for and contributions to building a better, more resilient financial system—a system that serves the real economy, by replacing those lost jobs and making up for that lost output.

> "Apart from a few mini-corrections and proposals for raising minimum levels of private capital for investment banks . . . absolutely nothing has happened in terms of serious regulation."

No Progress Has Been Made on Global Regulatory Reform

Lucas Zeise

Lucas Zeise is a writer for the Financial Times.

Despite the promises, there have been no meaningful financial reforms enacted in any country to address the financial crisis, Zeise maintains in the following viewpoint. Furthermore, the reform process is unduly influenced by a strong financial lobby that will block any serious attempts at reform. In Europe, those pressing for the centralization of banking supervision are ignoring the threats to democracy such a system could create.

As you read, consider the following questions:

1. How does the author suggest that governments can control the amount of credit a bank offers?

Lucas Zeise, "Banking Regulation? Malfunction!" This article was first published in German in *Blatter fur deutsche und internationale Politik* 2/2010 (www.blaetter.de) and has been provided by *Eurozine* (www.eurozine.com) Translation by Simon Garnett. Copyright © Lucas Zeise, Blatter fur deutsche und internationale Politik, Eurozine, February 5, 2010. Reproduced by permission.

2. The author suggests that there are at least some small steps being taken for financial reform. What are they?

3. The author applauds Iceland for its actions after the collapse of its banks. What position did the government take that the author states could halt deregulation?

Two years have passed since the outbreak of the property and financial crisis, yet there has been no progress in the regulation of the banking and financial sectors. Worse still, a serious start has not even been made. This diagnosis doesn't only go for Germany. It applies equally to the U.S., the European Union [EU], and at the level of international regulation.

Not that there has been a lack of fine words. Alongside U.S. president Barack Obama, who last summer [2009] announced the biggest "overhaul of the financial regulatory system since the reforms that followed the Great Depression", the German chancellor [Angela Merkel] is now proving to be a master of empty promises. Her new year's address of 2010 contained the beautiful sentence: "We must and will continue to work resolutely to introduce new rules into the financial markets, which will in the future prevent in good time the concentration of excess and irresponsibility." . . .

Cynics as Realists

Cynics will say that exactly this was foreseeable following the bank bailouts in autumn 2008, when practically all capitalist countries ensured the survival of "their" domestic banks with hundreds of billions of euros, dollars, yen and pounds. The cynics have turned out to be realists. They knew that the political establishment is always and everywhere closely associated with the most senior figures in the financial sector—or "high finance", as one used to say. They do not even need to mention in detail that the investment bank Goldman Sachs has the best possible connections in all the upper echelons of U.S. government, or that Germany's leading commercial bank

(Deutsche Bank) and leading insurance company (Allianz) have exercised a very strong influence on the legislative and executive since the beginning of the FRG [Federal Republic of Germany] (and of course before then, too). . . .

In terms of results, it all seems clear enough. Apart from a few mini-corrections and proposals for raising minimum levels of private capital for investment banks, which will be implemented in who knows how many years, nothing, absolutely nothing has happened in terms of serious regulation. In view of the economic disaster caused by financial speculation, that surely is surprising.

After all, an economic crisis, particularly one of this scale, is no fun for capitalists either. Not all managed to remain in the profit zone. More than a few had to file for bankruptcy. In fact, it ought to be in the interests of industrial and commercial capital—let's call it that rather than pure money capital or finance capital—to avoid similar occurrences in the future. In other words, there needs to be stricter state control of the financial sector. Otherwise financial crises will simply be unavoidable. Indeed, this conclusion seemed to have been reached by many people in many different places. However when it comes to concrete matters, the financial market becomes the judge of how regulation is carried out (which is what the neoliberal business model intends).

Banks' Obligations on Private Capital

Since banks are able to offer practically unlimited amounts of credit, and can thereby create money, capitalist states have tried to control and limit this credit creation in order to avoid precisely the kind of crisis like the current one. The most important means to do this are regulations on the amount of private capital a bank must have in reserve in relation to the volume of credit on offer. The total credit offered is thereby limited. The first internationally binding regulation on the private capital ratio, the so-called Basel Accord (Basel I), came into effect in 1988. In general, it stipulated an 8 per cent rule. In other words, 8 per cent of every loan offered by a bank had to be backed up by private capital, or, to put it another way, the banks were only allowed to loan out 12.5 times their own capital.

From the outset however, this agreement had holes in it. Worse, the rules were soon relaxed, supposedly in the interests of greater efficiency. After more than ten years of negotiations, the Basel II Accord came into effect in 2008, the year of the crisis. It ruled that a bank has to put aside a high amount of private capital for high-risk investments and low amount of private capital for low-risk investments. Basel II, in other words, meant that the banking supervisory body has to assess banks' increasingly complex risk-measurement systems, a task for which it is unequipped.

In December 2009, the Basel Committee on Banking Supervision—the body that Basel I and II had created—proposed raising the private capital requirements of banks. It also recommended that the concept of private capital be more narrowly defined. However, Basel II itself was not questioned. The committee wants to implement this gentle tightening of private capital regulations extremely cautiously, or at any rate not immediately. This considerateness follows the bidding of governments, who at the G-20 [a group of finance ministers from twenty countries who meet to discuss economic issues] meeting in April 2009 spoke out in favour of stricter regulations, however wanted them implanted only "after the crisis".

Early Warning System Out of Order

Still, it is possible to observe at least small signs of ideological progress in banking control. Governments recognize that they need an institution that takes care of financial stability. They are clearly not doing this job themselves, nor apparently do they see themselves in a position to start. For that reason, the "Financial Stability Forum" was tasked with acting as an early-

warning system at the international level. It is supposed to sound the alarm, to draw attention to flaws in the financial system, and to circulate suggestions for improvements if anything goes wrong. The forum was set up back in 1999, following the Asian crisis, which indicates its greatest shortcoming. Its first president was Hans Tietmeyer, who had recently retired as president of the German [Deutsche] Bundesbank. Under his leadership, the forum omitted to condemn the international speculation that had led to the hyper-boom in the Southeast Asian tiger states, and then to the flight of capital from the region in 1997, which left in its wake a serious economic crisis. Instead, the forum moaned about the poor statistics of the Asian national economies. Today, the forum is equally "competently" staffed as before—with eminent bankers, central bankers and bank supervisors.

Until now, a macroeconomy did not exist in Europe. There has also been no pan-European economic policy. The crisis has at least caused something to change in conceptual terms. A body has been installed equivalent to that at the global level in order to forecast instability and even to offer suggestions to governments. It is headed by none other than the president of the European Central Bank, currently the Frenchman Jean-Claude Trichet. Like the institution he leads, Trichet for a long time denied the existence of a financial crisis, and when denial was no longer possible, deemed its effect upon the remaining economy negligible. This new arrangement is sure to prove extremely useful for the citizens of the EU.

There are some remarkable parallels between the U.S. and Europe here. In both the world's two largest national economies, the intention is that the chaos and incompetence should be reduced somewhat; in both regions, the central banks will take control. Compared to the "diversity" of competence that currently dominates the field, that might be a marginal improvement. It is consistent, at any rate. As the creator of the dollar, the Fed [Federal Reserve System] can indeed rescue banks. It has recently been doing just this, with Élan [Financial Services]. However it is also consistent that control over private banks has been handed over to a state institution that nevertheless belongs to these banks.

In Europe, governments want to centralize the supervisory bodies that have until now been operating at the national level. A committee made up of representatives of the many national banking supervisory bodies will be formed to this end. Presiding over it will in turn be the president of the ECB [European Central Bank]. However what authority will the committee have when it comes to closing or bailing out a bank? Can it really order the national supervisory body of a country, against its own (government's) will, to do such a thing? One is almost grateful to the governments in London and Berlin that, at the instigation of their domestic banks, they refused to give this new body such a far-reaching mandate.

In Germany, too, the Bundesbank is in the process of extending its supervisory role. However neither it nor the CDU [Christian Democratic Union]-led government can argue with the economic crisis. In its analysis of the crisis, as well as in its bailout measures, the Bundesbank has proved itself to be extraordinarily incompetent. That such an important area of state activity should be handed over to an institution that is beyond parliamentary control is a further step towards the de-democratization of the country.

The Same Procedure?

In derivatives[1] trading, too, the finance lobby is in the process of asserting itself across a broad front. In order to avoid similar accusations that followed the Lehman [Brothers, a global financial services firm] collapse, so-called "central counterparties" have now been installed. They act as a general market central. If a bank collapses, they take over its contracts. The creditworthiness of these institutions must be beyond all doubt. A state-protected institution is the only option. The result: The state acts as guarantor of the speculation business. In terms of the limitation of speculation itself, on the other hand, there is nothing to speak of.

While the ratings agencies were indeed given a sharp ticking off shortly after the outbreak of the crisis, there is still no sign of a reform. They are neither controlled, nor has their power been reduced. On the contrary: The ratings agencies bear some of the responsibility for the disastrous way Greece's debt crisis has been handled. Not only banks, but also governments have referred to their judgments as if they were law. This scandal is continuing completely unchecked.

True, there could soon be a register for all hedge funds.[2] However, control of this currently rather unsuccessful sector is nonexistent.

Moreover, the free circulation of capital is not even seen as a problem. As decoration, one might also mention that the German Social Democrats as well as Britain's Labour prime minister Gordon Brown are currently backing the old call for a financial transactions tax—probably because they know that it will never happen. Governments appear not to be bothered by the fact that mass carry-trade (acquiring debt in currencies with low interest rates while investing in highly profitable currencies) not only distorts the market, but also runs contrary to the intended effect of the financial policies.

The Icelandic Example

Symptomatic of the failure of state actors is the conflict over the repayment of the money that, using high interest rates as a lure, Icelandic banks amassed from British, Dutch and German savers prior to 2008. Back then, the guest countries, in accordance with EU law, decided not to impose their national investment security systems on the Icelandic banks. The deregulatory principle of freedom of establishment, disastrous in every relationship, ruled. In other words, the EU member states quite consciously opted not to protect their citizens from the unserious financial deals offered by these banks. In 2008, the three Icelandic banks finally collapsed, and the remains were nationalized.

The UK [United Kingdom], Dutch and German governments have compensated their conned citizens and want the Icelandic state to foot this bill (3.8 billion euros) according to a contract drawn up with Iceland. However, after the Icelanders staged massive protests, the president Ólafur Grímsson refused to ratify it. A popular referendum will now take place that is very likely to reject this law.

One can only applaud the Icelanders and their president. By refusing to take responsibility for the losses incurred by the banks and the speculators, the Icelandic people have probably found the sole effective lever for halting deregulation—and ultimately even reversing it.

Notes

1. Derivatives have no underlying financial worth but are instead financial products whose worth is based on changes in the value of the underlying asset. Underlying assets usually consist of stocks or groupings of stocks in an index, a specific financial event, interest rates, or commodities. Participants in derivatives are essentially wagering that the asset will either grow or decline, and will be paid, or lose their investment, based on the behavior of the asset.

2. A hedge fund is a private investment pool characterized by unconventional investment methods and minimal regulation. These funds typically undertake balanced risks to ensure profit regardless of market conditions.

> *"Above all, Canada's experience seems to support those who say that the way to keep banking safe is to keep it boring—that is, to limit the extent to which banks can take on risk."*

Canada's Banking Regulations Created a Stable Banking System

Paul Krugman

Paul Krugman is a professor of economics and international affairs at Princeton University and an op-ed columnist at the New York Times. *He won the Nobel Prize in Economics in 2008. A self-described liberal, Krugman is the author or editor of more than twenty books.*

The U.S. banking system could benefit from adopting some of the principles used in Canadian banking, according to Krugman in the following viewpoint. Although both the United States and Canada have faced in recent years similar economic challenges—a trade imbalance with Asia and a flood of cheap money from Asia—their responses were different. Essentially, what Canada did right was to keep banking boring—to limit the amount of risk a bank can take on. Canada did this by placing limits on banks' debt levels and regulating the process of securitization.

As you read, consider the following questions:

1. During the banking crisis, what were some of the events that occurred in the United States that didn't occur in Canada?

2. In what way does Canada refute the view that the crisis was caused by the existence of financial institutions that were "too big to fail"?

3. Does Krugman believe the United States will enact measures to adopt a banking system more like Canada's? Why or why not?

In times of crisis, good news is no news. Iceland's meltdown made headlines; the remarkable stability of Canada's banks, not so much.

Yet as the world's attention shifts from financial rescue to financial reform, the quiet success stories deserve at least as much attention as the spectacular failures. We need to learn from those countries that evidently did it right. And leading that list is our neighbor to the north. Right now, Canada is a very important role model.

Yes, I know, Canada is supposed to be dull. The *New Republic* famously pronounced "Worthwhile Canadian Initiative" (from a *Times* op-ed column in the '80s) the world's most boring headline. But I've always considered Canada fascinating, precisely because it's similar to the United States in many but not all ways. The point is that when Canadian and U.S. experience diverge, it's a very good bet that policy differences, rather than differences in culture or economic structure, are responsible for that divergence.

And anyway, when it comes to banking, boring is good.

Limiting Banking Risk Is the Key

First, some background. Over the past decade [2000–2009] the United States and Canada faced the same global environment. Both were confronted with the same flood of cheap goods and cheap money from Asia. Economists in both countries cheerfully declared that the era of severe recessions was over.

But when things fell apart, the consequences were very different here and there. In the United States, mortgage defaults soared, some major financial institutions collapsed, and others survived only thanks to huge government bailouts. In Canada, none of that happened. What did the Canadians do differently?

It wasn't interest rate policy. Many commentators have blamed the Federal Reserve [the Fed] for the financial crisis, claiming that the Fed created a disastrous bubble by keeping interest rates too low for too long. But Canadian interest rates have tracked U.S. rates quite closely, so it seems that low rates aren't enough by themselves to produce a financial crisis.

Canada's experience also seems to refute the view, forcefully pushed by Paul Volcker, the formidable former Fed chairman, that the roots of our crisis lay in the scale and scope of our financial institutions—in the existence of banks that were "too big to fail." For in Canada essentially all the banks are too big to fail: just five banking groups dominate the financial scene.

On the other hand, Canada's experience does seem to support the views of people like Elizabeth Warren, the head of the congressional panel overseeing the bank bailout, who place much of the blame for the crisis on failure to protect consumers from deceptive lending. Canada has an independent Financial Consumer Agency, and it has sharply restricted subprime-type lending [which is risky for lenders and expensive for credit-poor borrowers].

Above all, Canada's experience seems to support those who say that the way to keep banking safe is to keep it boring—that is, to limit the extent to which banks can take on risk. The United States used to have a boring banking system, but [President Ronald] Reagan-era deregulation made things dangerously interesting. Canada, by contrast, has maintained a happy tedium.

More specifically, Canada has been much stricter about limiting banks' leverage, the extent to which they can rely on borrowed funds. It has also limited the process of securitization, in which banks package and resell claims on their loans outstanding—a process that was supposed to help banks reduce their risk by spreading it, but has turned out in practice to be a way for banks to make ever-bigger wagers with other people's money.

There's no question that in recent years these restrictions meant fewer opportunities for bankers to come up with clever ideas than would have been available if Canada had emulated America's deregulatory zeal. But that, it turns out, was all to the good.

Can the United States Learn from Canada?

So what are the chances that the United States will learn from Canada's success?

Actually, the financial reform bill that the House of Representatives passed in December [2009] would significantly Canadianize the U.S. system. It would create an independent Consumer Financial Protection Agency; it would establish limits on leverage; and it would limit securitization by requiring that lenders hold on to some of their loans.

But prospects for a comparable bill getting the 60 votes now needed to push anything through the Senate are doubtful. Republicans are deafly dead set against any significant financial reform—not a single Republican voted for the House bill—and some Democrats are ambivalent, too.

So there's a good chance that we'll do nothing, or nothing much, to prevent future banking crises. But it won't be because we don't know what to do: We've got a clear example of how to keep banking safe sitting right next door.

"It is now clear that the government at the time committed a classic mistake in deregulation, allowing the financial sector to undertake high-risk activities without adequate regulatory structure."

The Deregulation of Iceland's Banks Led to a Financial Crisis

Jon Danielsson and Gylfi Zoega

Jon Danielsson is a scholar of finance at the London School of Economics and Political Science, and Gylfi Zoega is a scholar of economics at Birkbeck College.

The collapse of Iceland's banking system is unlikely to be duplicated elsewhere, because a unique set of circumstances came together in Iceland to create a perfect storm that led to a systemic failure, according to Danielsson and Zoega in the following viewpoint. Several years ago, Iceland decided to transform its economy to one heavily dependent upon international banking, becoming what the authors term a "hedge fund sitting in the middle of the North Atlantic." To create a favorable climate for banking, the country privatized and deregulated its banking sys-

Jon Danielsson and Gylfi Zoega, "Entranced by Banking," *Vox*, February 9, 2009. Copyright © 2009 VoxEU.org. Reproduced by permission.

*tem. Banks came under the control of business-oriented indi-
viduals with little banking expertise, the authors explain.
Iceland's banks began engaging in high-risk activities with virtually no regulatory oversight. As a result, these banks were doomed
to fail, even if the global financial crisis had not occurred, the
authors contend.*

As you read, consider the following questions:

1. What are the three elements that the authors contend
   came together to create a "perfect storm" that created
   the failure of Iceland's banks?

2. What reasons do the authors give for saying that the
   role models for banking in countries such as Luxembourg and Switzerland were inappropriate for Iceland?

3. In the authors' opinion, why might pan-European regulations coupled with national enforcement be problematic?

Iceland underwent a systemic crisis in October last year
[2008], the only developed economy to do so in recent decades. The fate of Iceland is sometimes taken as an indication
of what might happen to other countries with an outsized financial sector, such as the UK [United Kingdom]. However,
the main factors in Iceland's downfall can be explained by its
unique history, inappropriate policy responses, and weaknesses in EU [European Union] banking regulations, conspir-
ing to make a perfect storm, unlikely to happen elsewhere.
Our study of the Icelandic collapse, available here, provides
the details.

Traditionally, the Icelandic economy was more regulated
and politicized than economies in most other Western countries. Economic management was more based on discretion
than rules, with tight connections between private sector firms
and political parties. The banking system was politicised with
access to capital based on nepotism and political connections.

Government control over the economy has reduced over time, with key events being the joining of the European Free Trade Association and then the European Economic Area [EEA] in the early 1990s. The latter meant that Iceland got extensive access to European markets and adopted European regulations.

Iceland did however retain to some extent its discretionary approach to economic management, and its key institutions, such that the Central Bank [of Iceland] and the financial regulator remained weaker than in most of its European counterparts.

Betting on Banking

The Icelanders decided a few years ago that their economic future lay in banking and privatised and deregulated their banking system. The banks passed into the hands of individuals with little experience of modern banking, while supervision remained weak.

The role models were easy to find, other small countries, such as Luxembourg and Switzerland have done quite well out of banking. What the Icelanders forgot was that those countries have centuries worth of experience running banks and the associated infrastructure, while Iceland has less than a decade.

The banks passed into the hands of individuals with extensive business interests. The result was a system of cross holdings, with liquidity needs being met within the group. The banks retained tight connections to the political superstructure.

The banks, with strong government support, proceeded to take advantage of ample capital in international markets to fuel high degrees of leverage [the use of debt to grow an investment] and exponential growth, eventually growing tenfold in just over four years to a size of about ten times the economy.

Iceland's institutional structure lagged behind developments in the banking sector. Neither the Central Bank nor the financial regulator developed the necessary infrastructure, nor did they receive the necessary independence and backup from the authorities to fulfill their duties adequately. This is manifested by the fact that while the assets of the banking system grew 900% as a fraction of GDP [gross domestic product] from 2003 to 2007, contributions to the financial regulator only grew by 47%.

It is now clear that the government at the time committed a classic mistake in deregulation, allowing the financial sector to undertake high-risk activities without adequate regulatory structure.

An Unstable Banking System

The growth in the banking system affected the entire economy, with many firms and even households adopting their business model of extreme leverage driving asset acquisitions.

The country decided to stake its economic future on international banking, with all of the inherent risks ignored. It did not have institutional structure to adequately supervise the banking system nor develop the ability to provide lending of last resort services.

Iceland was in effect turned into a hedge fund [a private investment pool characterized by unconventional investment methods and minimal regulation] sitting in the middle of the North Atlantic. It is not like the country was poor and needed high-risk activities to grow. Iceland was already an affluent economy and had reached the income per capita levels of Germany, France and the UK in year 2000 before the banking sector expanded.

The three main Icelandic banks were tightly interconnected. They did business with many of the same firms, were all dependent to a varying extent on the same macroeconomy, and were perceived by international capital markets as being highly related.

A difficulty in one bank directly affected confidence in the other banks, affecting access to liquidity [the ability of an asset to be quickly converted to cash without affecting the asset's price] and perhaps triggering bank runs. The three banks accounted for about 85% of Iceland's financial system and there was no doubt that their failure would have catastrophic effects for the Icelandic economy.

Eventually, their hubris caught up with them. The banks started having problems borrowing in wholesale markets and decided that opening up high interest savings accounts in the UK and elsewhere in Europe was a good idea. The Icelandic banks, with government permission, used European savers to provide the liquidity they could not obtain from the better-informed banking system.

Unheeded Warnings

There were ample warnings that something was amiss. In addition to papers and interviews with local economists, a natural starting point is a critical report from the Danske Bank [in 2006, titled "Iceland: Geyser Crisis"]. . . .

By contrast, official reports were more favourable. The *Financial Stability* report of the Central Bank of Iceland in (April 2008) indicated that the economy was in a good state. . . .

While documenting the strengths of the Icelandic economy was a worthwhile task and necessary for the maintenance of confidence in its banking system, such reports may have blinded policy makers to the coming storm.

The instability of the banking system appears to have caused little concerns from the authorities. Why this is the case is unclear. After all, both the financial regulator and the Central Bank had or should have had ample information on the stability of the banks as well as the legal ability and obligation to prevent destabilising banking.

The best explanation seems to be regulatory capture. This went as far as the financial regulator even participating in the Landsbanki's marketing of Internet accounts in the Netherlands only a few months before its collapse when it should have been clear that the bank was likely to fail.

If Banks Are Too Big to Save, Failure Is a Self-Fulfilling Prophecy

In this global crisis, the strength of a bank's balance sheet is of little consequence. What matters is the explicit or implicit guarantee provided by the state to the banks to back up their assets and provide liquidity. Therefore, the size of the state relative to the size of the banks becomes a crucial factor. If the banks become too big to save, their failure becomes a self-fulfilling prophecy.

The reasons for the failure of the Icelandic banks are in many ways similar to the difficulties experienced by many financial institutions globally, such as the seemingly unlimited access to cheap capital, excessive risk taking, and lax standards of risk management.

The crucial difference is scale. While many countries have their share of troubled banks, in those cases the problems are confined to only a segment of their banking system, in economies where the overall assets of the banks are much smaller relative to GDP. In those countries the government has adequate resources to contain the fallout from individual bank failures.

Ultimately this implies that the blame for bank failures lies at home rather than internationally. We suspect that even if the world had not entered into a serious financial crisis, the Icelandic banks would have failed.

Sweden's Financial Crisis Provides Lessons to the United States

Sweden's banking crisis [of the early 1990s] grew slowly over time and was the result of a number of policy decisions. In particular, the crisis arose from a set of economic policies that attempted to: 1) support Sweden's fixed exchange rate policy, 2) deregulate the financial sector, 3) expand credit, and 4) provide low-cost loans for residential purchases and for university students. Eventually, a drop in asset values weakened the balance sheets of banks and reduced liquidity in the economy. One key factor in Sweden's financial crisis was a set of policy measures the country adopted in the mid-1980s to liberalize the highly regulated financial sector. . . .

The Swedish experience may offer some insight into one possible way of resolving a domestic financial crisis. One factor that helped Sweden quickly resolve its financial crisis was a strong international economic recovery that pushed up real estate values in Sweden and improved the balance sheets of banks. Others argue that a number of procedural factors, in addition to the economic recovery, helped bring the financial crisis to a resolution.

James K. Jackson,
"The U.S. Financial Crisis: Lessons from Sweden,"
CRS Report for Congress, *September 29, 2008.*

Government's Response—Gambling for Resurrection

Given the ample warnings the government had of the pending difficulties in the banking system, its apparent lack of concern is surprising. Surely the regulator and the Central Bank knew what was happening.

The only public information we have has the Central Bank and the financial regulator blaming each other, with the government claiming not to have been informed, and blaming the global economy. We do not find this convincing. Such a catastrophic pending failure had to have been discussed by the entire Cabinet.

We therefore cannot escape the feeling that the board and directors of the Central Bank and the financial services authority, along with senior officials there knew what was happening. Similarly, all government ministers, along with senior bureaucrats in the ministries of finance, commerce, foreign affairs, and office of the prime minister had to have known.

Still the government failed to act. It could have at any point taken decisions that would have alleviated the eventual outcome. If the government had acted prudently the economy would have been left in a much better shape.

By not addressing the pending failure of the banking system, perhaps in the hope that the instability would disappear, we cannot escape the feeling that the Icelandic authorities gambled for resurrection, and failed.

Weaknesses in European Banking Regulations

Iceland's collapse also exposes fault lines in the EU/EEA approach to banking supervision. Regulations are Europe-wide, with supervision in the hands of the home regulator, which can be problematic in the case of cross-border banking if the host supervisor does not have the necessary information and responsibilities or does not cooperate adequately with the home supervisor.

Within the EU/EEA regulations are mostly pan-European, but supervision (enforcement) is national. This may lead to problems where authorities in one country see that other countries have the same regulations, and implicitly assume supervision is the same. Politically it is (currently) impossible to implement Europe-wide supervision.

A good example of problems that may arise is the high-interest savings accounts, Icesave, set up across Europe by Landsbanki, when it was having difficulties obtaining funds in wholesale markets. According to European Union laws, the home regulator is in charge of supervision and offers deposit insurance of at least €20,887, but the host supervisor may offer more, as is the case in the UK.

After the run on Northern Rock [a British bank], the UK government announced that no individual UK deposit holder would lose money in the case of bankruptcy. At the very least, this provided an implicit guarantee to Icesave depositors. In this case it would have been essential that the UK FSA [Financial Services Authority] also exercised supervisory duties. It is unclear to what extent this was done.

In addition, in the EU/EEA, deposit insurance is provided by a national insurance fund paid for by banks. It is unclear what is supposed to happen if the national insurance fund is not sufficient.

The authorisation of the opening of cross-border savings accounts of the magnitude and risk of Icesave represents a serious failure in the decision-making process by the supervisors in Iceland and the host countries, the UK and the Netherlands and/or in EU/EEA regulations.

The supervisors in all three countries should have recognised the dangers and acted to prevent the rapid expansion of Icesave. Ultimately, supervision failed. The notion that a country of 300,000 inhabitants could assume the responsibility of providing deposit insurance of the magnitude of Icesave is absurd.

We suspect this also casts light on another failure of cross-border banking supervision in Europe. Host supervisors generally only observed the part of the banks operating in their country, not the overall picture. Some of the Icelandic banks had extensive operations of various types both within Europe and outside.

Unless an individual national supervisor has a clear picture of those operations, it is difficult to exercise adequate supervision. The Icelandic regulator may have been the only supervisor that had the complete picture. If so, the only supervisor who had the necessary information failed.

Deregulation Was to Blame

The Icelandic economy crashed because the financial system was deregulated and privatised without adequate supervision; there was insufficient institutional knowledge, both within the banking system and within the government on how to run and regulate a modern banking system; and the government failed to recognise the systemic risk of having such a large banking system.

Ultimately, when the banks were heading for failure the government opted for gambling for resurrection rather than closing the banks down. The government's gamble failed and Iceland as a consequence suffered a systemic crisis.

Periodical Bibliography

The following articles have been selected to supplement the diverse views presented in this chapter.

Richard G. Anderson   "Resolving a Banking Crisis, the Nordic Way," *Economic Synopses*, February 18, 2009.

Carter Dougherty   "Stopping a Financial Crisis, the Swedish Way," *New York Times*, September 22, 2008.

Marc Levinson, as told to Roya Wolverson   "Financial Regulation Pitfalls," Council on Foreign Relations, October 28, 2009. www.cfr.org.

Greg Palast   "Confronting the Globalcrat," *Nation*, December 2, 2009.

Public Citizen   "The Connection Between the World Trade Organization's Extreme Financial Service Deregulation Requirements and the Global Economic Crisis," November 2009. www.citizen.org.

Andrew Purvis   "Sweden's Model Approach to Financial Disaster," *Time*, September 24, 2008.

Guy Sorman   "Whether It's Greece or the U.S., Statism Riskier than Free Market," *Investor's Business Daily*, March 22, 2010.

Nobusuke Tamaki   "Bank Regulation in Japan," *CESifo DICE Report*, vol. 6, no. 3, 2008.

Thomas Walkom   "So Much for the 'Free' Market. Now What? Faced with a Choice Between Chinese- or Swedish-Style Capitalism, Which Road Will U.S. Take?" *Toronto Star* (Canada), October 5, 2008.

Kamarul Yunus   "PM: We're Committed to Open Trade," *New Straits Times* (Malaysia), November 11, 2009.

For Further Discussion

Chapter 1

1. The repeal of the Glass-Steagall Act, which allowed commercial banks to also engage in investment banking activities, is seen by Joseph E. Stiglitz as a factor contributing to the financial crisis. Mark A. Calabria questions whether the act played a significant role. What reasons does each give for his conclusion?

2. The role of Ronald Reagan in setting the stage for the financial crisis is the subject of debate among commentators and analysts. In their respective viewpoints, Paul Krugman blames the deregulatory actions put in place during the Reagan presidency for the financial meltdown, while Stephen Spruiell defends Reagan. Citing the viewpoints, whose position do you find more compelling, and why?

Chapter 2

1. While both viewpoints agree that some financial regulation is needed in response to the financial crisis, Robert Hahn and Peter Passell call for a light touch, while Robert E. Litan presses for more sweeping reform. What are some of the major differences in their recommendations?

2. The role of the Federal Reserve in financial reform has been the topic of considerable debate. The current chairman of the Federal Reserve, Ben S. Bernanke, argues for an expanded role for the Federal Reserve, citing the expertise and experience of the board. Jeffrey A. Miron argues that the Federal Reserve had a role in causing the financial

crisis and should be eliminated, rather than given more powers. Whose argument do you find more compelling, and why?

Chapter 3

1. Although airlines have been deregulated since 1978, debate continues about the success of deregulation in the industry. Robert L. Crandall argues that more regulation is needed while Steven A. Morrison and Clifford Winston contend that further deregulation is needed. Citing from the viewpoints, identify which of these conflicting arguments you find more persuasive.

2. The success of deregulation of the electric power market is debated in Chapter 3, with Steven Pearlstein contending that deregulation has not benefitted consumers and Jerry Taylor and Peter Van Doren arguing that true deregulation would be beneficial to consumers. What are some of the assumptions about the electric power market that the authors share? What are some of the differences?

Chapter 4

1. Canada's economy has remained relatively stable following the global financial crisis. What are some of the factors responsible for the nation's stability? What can the United States learn from Canada regarding its own economy? Explain your answer.

2. The economy of Iceland has been severely challenged by the global economic crisis. What were some of the factors that fueled the crisis, and in your opinion, could the crisis have been avoided? Explain why or why not.

Organizations to Contact

The editors have compiled the following list of organizations concerned with all the issues debated in this book. The descriptions are derived from materials provided by the organizations. All have publications or information available for interested readers. The names, addresses, phone and fax numbers, and e-mail and Internet addresses may change. Be aware that many organizations take several weeks or longer to respond to inquiries, so allow as much time as possible.

American Economic Association (AEA)
2014 Broadway, Suite 305, Nashville, TN   37203
(615) 322-2595 • fax: (615) 343-7590
e-mail: aeainfo@vanderbilt.edu
Web site: www.vanderbilt.edu/AEA

The American Economic Association (AEA) is a scholarly organization composed of economists from academic, business, government, and other professional institutions. The association encourages economic research, issues publications on economic subjects, and encourages freedom of economic discussion. The AEA publishes the *American Economic Review*, the *Journal of Economic Literature*, the *Journal of Economic Perspectives*, and the *American Economic Journals*.

Bretton Woods Committee (BWC)
1726 M Street NW, Suite 200, Washington, DC   20036
(202) 331-1616 • fax: (202) 785-9423
e-mail: info@brettonwoods.org
Web site: www.brettonwoods.org

The Bretton Woods Committee (BWC) is a bipartisan group dedicated to increasing public understanding of international financial and development issues and the roles of the World Bank, International Monetary Fund, and World Trade Organization. Members include industry and financial leaders, economists, university leaders, and former government officials. On its Web site, BWC publishes the quarterly *BWC Newsletter* and reports, including *The United States and the WTO: Benefits of the Multilateral Trade System*.

Brookings Institution

1775 Massachusetts Avenue NW, Washington, DC 20036
(202) 797-6000 • fax: (202) 797-6004
e-mail: communications@brookings.edu
Web site: www.brookings.edu

The Brookings Institution is a nonpartisan, nonprofit public policy think tank. Its mission is to conduct independent research and to provide innovative and practical recommendations that advance three broad goals, which include strengthening American democracy; fostering the economic and social welfare, security, and opportunity of all Americans; and securing a more open, safe, prosperous, and cooperative international system. The Economic Studies Program monitors the global economy and seeks answers to economic policy issues in the United States and abroad. The Brookings Institution publishes books, journals, and policy papers and makes newsletters, research, commentary, and podcasts available on its Web site. It has published literature on the topic of deregulation, including "Extending Deregulation: Make the U.S. Economy More Efficient."

Cato Institute

1000 Massachusetts Avenue NW
Washington, DC 20001-5403
(202) 842-0200 • fax: (202) 842-3490
e-mail: cato@cato.org
Web site: www.cato.org

The Cato Institute is a libertarian public policy research foundation dedicated to limiting the role of government and protecting individual liberties. It publishes books; journals, including the *Cato Journal* and the *Cato Policy Report*; opinion pieces; commentaries; testimonies; and speeches. Most of these are available on the institute's Web site. Some of the Cato Institute's areas of research are finance, banking, and monetary policy. Among its publications on deregulation is "The Deregulation of the Electricity Industry: A Primer."

Center for Economic and Policy Research (CEPR)
1611 Connecticut Avenue NW, Suite 400
Washington, DC 20009
(202) 293-5380 • fax: (202) 588-1356
e-mail: cepr@cepr.net
Web site: www.cepr.net

The Center for Economic and Policy Research (CEPR) is a progressive economic policy think tank that does research on social security, the U.S. housing bubble, developing country economies, and gaps in the social policy fabric of the U.S. economy. The mission of the CEPR is to promote democratic debate on economic and social issues. CEPR conducts both professional research and public education. The organization provides reports and briefing papers on its Web site. Among its publications on deregulation are "A Short History of Financial Deregulation in the United States" and a series of reports titled "Monitoring European Deregulation."

G-20 (Group of Twenty)
e-mail: g20uk.publicenquiries@hm-treasury.gov.uk
Web site: www.g20.org

The G-20, or Group of Twenty, is an informal forum of finance ministers and central bank governors from twenty industrialized and developing nations that meets to promote open and constructive discussion on key issues relating to global economic stability. By contributing to the strengthening of the international financial architecture and providing opportunities for dialogue on national policies, international cooperation, and international financial institutions, the G-20 helps to support growth and development across the globe. Case studies, reports, and other publications are available on its Web site.

Heritage Foundation

214 Massachusetts Avenue NE, Washington, DC   20002-4999
(202) 546-4400 • fax: (202) 546-0904
e-mail: info@heritage.org
Web site: www.heritage.org

The Heritage Foundation is a conservative think tank that supports the principles of free enterprise and limited government. Its many publications include the quarterly magazine the *Insider*, as well as frequent reports and Web memos. One of the institute's areas of research is enterprise and free markets, and it provides research, commentary, blogs, and charts on this topic on its Web site. Among a number of articles on deregulation is "Did Deregulation Cause the Wall Street Crisis?"

Hudson Institute (HI)

1015 Fifteenth Street NW, 6th Floor, Washington, DC   20005
(202) 974-2400 • fax: (202) 974-2410
e-mail: info@hudson.org
Web site: www.hudson.org

The Hudson Institute (HI) is a conservative think tank engaged in research and analysis to promote global security, prosperity, and freedom and to advise global leaders in government and business. The future-oriented institute undertakes interdisciplinary and collaborative studies in defense, international relations, economics, culture, science, technology, and law. Articles, papers, an electronic newsletter, reports, speeches, and testimonies are available on the institute's Web site.

International Monetary Fund (IMF)

700 Nineteenth Street NW, Washington, DC   20431
(202) 623-7000 • fax: (202) 623-4661
e-mail: publicaffairs@imf.org
Web site: www.imf.org

The International Monetary Fund (IMF) is an international organization of 184 member countries. It was established to promote international monetary cooperation, exchange stability, and orderly exchange arrangements. IMF seeks to foster economic growth and high levels of employment and provides temporary financial assistance to countries. It publishes the quarterly *Finance & Development* as well as reports on its activities, including the quarterly *Global Financial Stability Report*. Recent issues of the report, data on IMF finances, and individual country reports are available on the IMF's Web site.

Peterson Institute for International Economics (IIE)

1750 Massachusetts Avenue NW, Washington, DC 20036
(202) 328-9000 • fax: (202) 659-3225
Web site: www.iie.com

The Peterson Institute for International Economics (IIE) is a private, nonprofit, nonpartisan research organization devoted to the study of international economic policy. Its agenda emphasizes global macroeconomic topics, international money and finance, trade and related social issues, energy and the environment, investment, and domestic adjustment policies. Current priorities of the institute are the global financial and economic crisis; globalization; international trade imbalances and currency relationships; the competitiveness of the United States and other major countries; reform of the international economic and financial architecture; sovereign wealth funds; and trade negotiations at the multilateral, regional, and bilateral levels. The institute publishes books and papers on economic issues and makes policy briefs, working papers, speeches, testimonies, and commentaries available on its Web site. It publishes frequently on deregulation, including "Peterson Perspectives: A Step Forward on Financial Regulation."

World Bank

1818 H Street NW, Washington, DC 20433
(202) 473-1000 • fax: (202) 477-6391
e-mail: wbannualreport@worldbank.org
Web site: www.worldbank.org

The World Bank was established by the United Nations to reduce poverty and improve the standard of living of poor people around the world. It promotes sustainable growth and investments in developing countries through loans, technical assistance, and policy guidance. The bank makes documents and reports available via its Web site and issues policy papers on deregulation, including "Banking Deregulation and Industry Structure."

World Trade Organization

Rue de Lausanne 154, Geneva 21   CH-1211
   Switzerland
(41) 22 739 5111 • fax: (41) 22 731 42 06
e-mail: enquiries@wto.org
Web site: www.wto.org

The World Trade Organization (WTO) is an international organization with a purpose to create a framework of rules facilitating trade among nations. The goal of the organization is to "help producers of goods and services, exporters, and importers conduct their business." The WTO publishes numerous books, CD-ROMs, and reports that provide statistics and research on world trade.

Bibliography of Books

Viral Acharya and Matthew Richardson, eds.
Restoring Financial Stability: How to Repair a Failed System. Hoboken, NJ: John Wiley & Sons, 2009.

Andreas Busch
Banking Regulation and Globalization. New York: Oxford University Press, 2009.

Charles W. Calomiris
U.S. Bank Deregulation in Historical Perspective. New York: Cambridge University Press, 2006.

Alessandro Cento
The Airline Industry. New York: Springer Heidelberg, 2008.

Byron L. Dorgan
Reckless! How Debt, Deregulation, and Dark Money Nearly Bankrupted America (and How We Can Fix It!). New York: Thomas Dunne Books, 2009.

Carl Felsenfeld
International Banking Regulation. Huntington, NY: Juris Publishers, 2007.

John Bellamy Foster and Fred Magdoff
The Great Financial Crisis: Causes and Consequences. New York: Monthly Review Press, 2009.

Edward F. Greene et al.
U.S. Regulation of the International Securities and Derivatives Markets. Frederick, MD: Aspen Publishers, 2009.

James M. Griffin and Steven L. Puller, eds.	*Electricity Deregulation: Choices and Challenges*. Chicago, IL: University of Chicago Press, 2005.
Peter Z. Grossman and Daniel H. Cole, eds.	*The End of a Natural Monopoly: Deregulation and Competition in the Electric Power Industry*. Boston: JAI Press, 2003.
Richard F. Hirsh	*Power Loss: The Origins of Deregulation and Restructuring in the American Electric Utility System*. Cambridge, MA: MIT Press, 1999.
Leng Jing	*Corporate Governance and Financial Reform in China's Transition Economy*. Hong Kong: Hong Kong University Press, 2009.
Paul L. Joskow	*Deregulation: Where Do We Go from Here?* Washington, DC: AEI Press, 2009.
Alfred E. Kahn	*Lessons from Deregulation: Telecommunications and Airlines After the Crunch*. Washington, DC: Brookings Institution Press, 2004.
Andrew N. Kleit, ed.	*Electric Choices: Deregulation and the Future of Electric Power*. Lanham, MD: Rowman & Littlefield, 2006.
Paul W. MacAvoy	*The Unsustainable Costs of Partial Deregulation*. New Haven, CT: Yale University Press, 2007.

Donato
Masciandaro, ed.
Financial Intermediation in the New Europe: Banks, Markets, and Regulation in EU Accession Countries. Northampton, MA: Edward Elgar Publishers, 2004.

Kevin Phillips
Bad Money: Reckless Finance, Failed Politics, and the Global Crisis of American Capitalism. New York: Viking, 2008.

Colin Read
Global Financial Meltdown: How We Can Avoid the Next Economic Crisis. New York: Palgrave Macmillan, 2009.

Rothman School of Management
The Financial Crisis and Rescue: What Went Wrong? Why? What Lessons Can Be Learned? Toronto, Ontario, Canada: University of Toronto Press, 2008.

Peter Schweizer
Architects of Ruin: How Big Government Liberals Wrecked the Global Economy—and How They Will Do It Again If No One Stops Them. New York: HarperCollins, 2009.

Jagdish N. Sheth, Fred C. Allvine, Can Uslay, and Ashutosh Dixit
Deregulation and Competition: Lessons from the Airline Industry. Thousand Oaks, CA: Sage Publications, 2007.

John B. Taylor
Getting Off Track: How Government Actions and Interventions Caused, Prolonged, and Worsened the Financial Crisis. Stanford, CA: Hoover Institution Press, 2009.

| UNCTAD Secretariat Task Force on Systemic Issues and Economic Cooperation | *The Global Economic Crisis: Systemic Failures and Multilateral Remedies.* New York: United Nations, 2009. |
| Elmus Wicker | *The Great Debate on Banking Reform: Nelson Aldrich and the Origins of the Fed.* Columbus, OH: Ohio State University Press, 2008. |

Index